THE GIRL WHO WASN'T ME

A Memoir

Persephone Grey

This work is a memoir. It reflects the author's present recollection of her experiences over a period of years. Certain names, locations, and identifying characteristics have been changed. Dialogue and events have been recreated from memory, and, in some cases, have been compressed to convey the substance of what was said or what occurred. Some scenes are composites of events, and the timeline for some events has been compressed.

For the amazing humans who have been a part of my journey. You saw and loved me, and that made all the difference. May we always find beauty in our shadows.

Prologue

Growing up, I didn't have the language to describe my mom's moods; her obsessions, sadness, and anger. My mom was distant, charismatic, and highly manipulative to those closest to her. I don't remember her ever hugging me.

I still struggle to understand what happened to me. My childhood was so volatile, so shaky. The only way I was able to cope before was to pretend like it didn't happen, as if my life actually started in high school. After I moved out.

When people would get close to me, I would hold them at arm's length. I felt I had to bury my past. I didn't know how to communicate what happened to me in a way that didn't leave me feeling weak and vulnerable. I feared if they knew me, they would feel sorry for me. I could never live with that.

Any type of emotional intimacy made me feel physically ill. When I came out, I thought that might change things but that wasn't the big issue for me. That wasn't what was holding me back from getting close to someone. There was so much layered on top of my sexual identity that I needed to work through, and I was not yet equipped to deal with it. I realized that it was safer to be alone, to keep my past hidden from everyone, even myself.

I was in my late-20's when my mom was diagnosed with Asperger's. (Note: My mom was diagnosed in 2007. In 2013, the diagnosis of Asperger's was removed from the Diagnostic and Statistical Manual of Mental Disorders. People who have these symptoms are included within the autism spectrum disorder along with autism and pervasive developmental disorder not otherwise specified.)

I ran some internet searches and found there was a category for my situation; *neurotypical children of Asperger parents*. Reading other stories was like putting glasses on and seeing my life clearly for the first time. I hadn't just experienced abuse, there had always been *something else* under the surface.

I believe more research needs to be done on the psychological effects children experience growing up with an undiagnosed parent on the spectrum. I've only been able to find one scientific research paper, in contrast to the mountains of studies for parents with children on the spectrum. Even though I have come to learn that there are many of us out there. We stumble across each other in the comments sections from a handful of articles found. We cautiously share our stories. The experience both terrifying and exhilarating.

The more I discovered over the years, the more I was able to unbox myself, and come to terms with my childhood experiences- the escalating emotional and physical violence. I don't fault the autistic spectrum disorder for my mom's intentional actions, I have empathy towards her childhood experience. It was terrible, and unfortunately, she continued the cycle. But I won't discount what I went through, and I can't stop looking for answers.

I've tried to ask her why she did certain things, and if she ever loved me. Though I have asked her so many times over the years, I've come to accept that she isn't able to answer these questions for me.

And then, there is my dad.

1

I have lived in forty-two homes in seven different states. I am still not sure where I belong or who I belong to. Is it nowhere and no one? Or everywhere and everyone?

There are days when I turn the lights off, close the curtains against the sunshine, and know with certainty that there is only a deep darkness that will engulf us all.

Then I have days so bright and long that it feels like Alaska in the summertime. Everything is so vibrant and beautiful that I can't remember the dull ache of nothingness.

How are these two sides so clever at making me forget life with the other?

For a long time, I avoided thinking about my past because I could not (would not) remember. The early years blurred against my closed eyelids; the people I traveled with remained faceless.

I did have one faint memory that tugged at me, that when tugged back began to quickly unravel. I was in middle school. My mom used to tell me I was adopted, so she didn't have baby pictures of me. I felt she was lying but wasn't sure *why* she would do that. She always had a slight twist of the lips when she told me, but only she knew the punchline.

I'd roll my eyes at her response, not quite understanding how cruel she was being. I tried to play her game and act like I was in on her secret joke. I knew there were photo albums somewhere. I had seen glimpses of them, even though they seemed to move in the middle of the night those times I tried to find them.

In high school, after I had moved out, I asked my mom for a baby picture of myself for my senior yearbook page (one cannot underestimate the need to fit in as a teenager).

It was an emotionally dangerous mission, but I was determined. I went over to her place and after a tense negotiation, she agreed to give some to me.

If I went on birth control, I could have my baby pictures. These were her terms. I agreed, even though I was still a virgin.

To ask for something from her meant that I would have to sacrifice something important to me. The stakes getting higher with each step I took away from her, with each inch of control she thought she lost over me.

My mom would make an appointment within days and I would go. It never occurred to me that she wouldn't know whether I took the pills or not. By this time, I was conditioned to not even *consider* risking it.

With the deal made, she pointed me to a corner in the house and I spotted an album under a pile of books. Feeling vindicated that it existed, I quickly left her house with it tucked under my arm. This would be the first time I would see pictures of my young parents, of me from all those years ago.

After selecting a baby picture for the yearbook, I put the album away for a long time. But I eventually allowed myself to look through those yellowing Polaroids, maybe once or twice a year around the holidays or my birthday, the faces of my parents becoming blurry as I strained my eyes trying to recognize them, as I blinked back unwanted tears.

I'd grab a whiskey bottle and will them to come to life and speak to me. A few swigs later, I'd plead, "Who are you?" and impatiently wait for an answer.

Other times I'd draft separate emails to each parent: "I'm just writing to remind you that you have a daughter" or "I'm sorry" or "I hate you and hope you can't sleep at night." I'd wake up the next morning unsure if I sent the emails, feeling a pit in my stomach if I saw a reply from them. Feeling rejected if I didn't.

Those moments, those moods would paralyze me for days, so I tried to focus only on the present. I tried to pretend like the past wasn't chasing me day and night, relentlessly following me into my dreams and giving me anxiety the moment I woke up. My heart crashed against my rib cage before my eyes even had the chance to open.

I have always been able to hide this side of me, leaning on routine and OCD behavior to create a sense of normalcy in my day-to-day. I knew enough to fit in and to *get me through*. But I only had basic coping mechanisms, and as I grew older, I had to find other modes of survival. The most constructive was to be a workaholic. The worst, an inspiring alcoholic.

If you met me then, you would say I was kind, funny, and engaging. You would want to hang out with me, be in my orbit. You would think I was smart, confident, and ambitious. No matter your preference, you would find me sexy. If I was drinking whiskey, you would laugh at my jokes, yet feel stung when they were about you. But you would still call me, still love me.

My life sat upon a shaky balancing scale. I was the shifting of grains, going from one pile to the other. I went back and forth, everything to nothing, endlessly it seemed.

I was exhausted.

My thirty-fifth birthday was approaching, and a profound sadness settled over me. I had a vague understanding of my need for self-medication, my insatiable desire to be loved, and the dull response toward those who tried to give it to me. I was barely keeping my head above water; I barely felt joy anymore.

Everything happens for a reason. In the depths of this dark time, an opportunity came up with work for me to transfer to San Francisco. After building a life in the Washington, DC area for twenty years (excluding a short exodus to North Carolina in my mid-twenties), it seemed to be an option I would never consider. DC was my home, where I had worked hard to plant roots after a volatile childhood. I had the best of friends, the best times of my life there. But somehow, it felt necessary. So, I went.

I knew it would be hard moving away from my home, but I didn't understand just how alien the change would feel. In California, I felt lost in the moments between work and sleep, time stretched like putty. I was sober more often because I didn't like to drink alone, and I was alone because I didn't know many people.

The space around me suddenly seemed vast. I wasn't crowded by other happy hour patrons or squeezed onto a couch with friends. I wasn't taking in everyone else's daily detailed account of their lives. In the calm, I started to unpack the thoughts in my head, carefully placing and organizing them around me. A few memories multiplied into hundreds. Each detail like a stitch, sewing me back together.

2

My mom's dad, grandpa Lorenzo, was a first-generation Sicilian, born and raised in Chicago. He was tall, dark, and handsome, and when he entered a room, he was quick to dominate the space. You wanted to be noticed by him but then felt slightly uneasy if you were. Grandpa Lorenzo had his eye on your every move and was ready to build you up or knock you down depending on his mood.

I saw *The Godfather* when I was ten and became convinced that we had mob ties. Didn't all Sicilians? I was sure that I was a Sicilian princess and once the higher ups realized what was happening to me, they would take me away from my mom and send me to my homeland to play in the vineyards. I was wide-eyed and projected all my loving attention onto my grandpa Lorenzo so he would tell me stories validating my suspicions.

But I heard only one story which, even if true, was lame. He said that one summer he was paid to drive a car from Chicago to

Miami and instructed to not open the trunk. It hardly sounded like he had any pull. I crossed that off my list of escape plans and, as the years unfolded, I would come to understand that *he* was the source of what I was trying to escape.

My grandpa Lorenzo worked in personnel at the State Department. The position took him around the world as he hired civilian employees, handled complaints, and other such HR matters. In the '50s, due to the Korean war, he was sent to Seoul. The country had been ravaged by the war, the people starving and poor. It was one of the darkest times in Korea's history.

It was there that he met my grandma Grace. Back then her name was Soon. She changed her name when they moved to the States. She would change many things about herself, but it was necessary for her survival.

My grandma Grace had escaped North Korea during the war, alongside her mother, brothers, and sisters. Her father abandoned them, and her mother was frail. For years, my grandma Grace worked to feed, clothe, and shelter her younger siblings. Many days they had nothing more to eat than a few moldy potatoes. Meeting my grandpa Lorenzo must have seemed to be a dream come true.

They married in Seoul and eventually gave birth to two daughters. My aunt Sarah came first, and my mom followed a couple of years later. Neither of them has many memories of their time there and after my grandpa Lorenzo relocated them to the States, they lost their connection with Korea.

Fond stories of my mom's childhood are hard to come by. Life was never great, as my grandpa Lorenzo was abusive and controlling. My grandma Grace finally left him when the girls were in high school. He beat her badly one day and my aunt Sarah, summoning every bold fiber in her body, grabbed a baseball bat and threatened to hit him if he did not stop. Through a haze of alcohol and rage, even he could understand my aunt meant what she said, and he backed away. That event left the women shaky yet exhilarated. Standing up to my grandpa Lorenzo was like screaming into the face of a lion.

But there would be consequences.

My grandma Grace had no resources at that time to hire a good lawyer and so my grandpa Lorenzo was granted full custody and continued to move the girls around. His career took them around the world, and it was hard for my grandma Grace to keep in touch.

She stayed behind in Virginia and it would be quite some time before they reconnected.

My aunt looks back on that time as a wild adventure, even though their home life was quickly deteriorating. She was popular and could quickly adapt to new situations. She loved the exotic places they would move to. But my mom was a socially awkward bookworm. She struggled as they constantly moved, putting more time into her studies than in making friends.

My aunt's act of bravery had evened the playing field of my grandpa Lorenzo's abuse. She detached from him as she continued to live under his roof and then moved out as soon as she could, leaving my mom alone with him. My mom tried to be invisible. She hid behind musty books and large Coke-bottle glasses. But he sought her out, relentless in his desire to control someone.

3

My dad grew up in a small town in Ohio, born from second generation parents. His father's family had immigrated mostly from Romania while his mother's family immigrated from the Czech Republic. They were salt of the earth and worked as farmers, factory workers, and butchers. They were funny, creative and a deeply bonded family- living just houses apart if not in the same house.

My dad's parents, grandpa Joseph and grandma Emma, met in high school. He was boyishly handsome with a lean muscular build and dark, captivating eyes. She stood petite next to him, her Czech features soft and delicate on her face. She was quite stylish and favored brightly colored dresses and short shorts in the summer. They were both dashing and charismatic, and enjoyed the chase that led to their marriage.

My grandpa Joseph would rise to be the head of the county hospital and a well-respected influencer. My grandma Emma settled into the role of a housewife and hostess extraordinaire. After living in the suburbs for the first few years, they built a homestead on sixteen acres of land on the outskirts of the city. Their growing family had plenty of space to play, swim, and hunt. Deep in the woods there were even small waterfalls cascading from the creek down the steep, rocky hills.

This grandpa was also controlling and ran the house as he saw fit. My grandma Emma wanted to please him but there was always something not quite right and she never seemed to be enough for him. She battled her anxiety with morning, afternoon, and evening cocktails. She walked around with a coffee cup during the day filled with whatever alcohol was on hand and switched to appropriate glassware as evening settled in. For quite some time, she was able to hide her drinking. They entertained frequently and she would pull bottles from the cases meant for guests and hide them around the house for future consumption.

When the kids were in high school, my grandpa Joseph was around less frequently, leaving my grandma Emma to raise three boys and one girl. He had a not-so-secret family on the side. I met my half-aunt once. We were very close in age. She showed me her pet rock collection.

Back at the homestead, life moved forward. The kids were rambunctious, popular, and smart. The boys were athletic gods, dominating the school's wrestling team. My aunt rode the tail of their successes but was equally charismatic in her own right. The siblings came and went on their motorcycles and trucks, often having friends over to build bonfires and party into the night. My grandma Emma's youngest child would be born some time later, only a few years before me. We would grow up like sisters.

4

When Mom was seventeen, her father received an assignment in Germany. He had reached elevated levels of frustration, as he could neither get a rise out of her, nor break her. As he pushed, she only became more depressed and withdrawn. My grandpa Lorenzo decided the best way to crack my mom was to check her into the psychiatric ward at the Army base.

My dad was twenty-two years old and a counselor in the Army. He was interested in medicine but didn't have the internal motivation pushing him toward a college degree, so he had joined the Army and served for a few years. He was a few months away from becoming a civilian again when this shy, beautiful girl walked into his office. She poured her heart and soul out to him. Nobody had listened to her before. Drawing had been one of her only outlets. My dad was an empathetic man—sensitive and caring. He was moved by my mom, and as they spent more time together, they fell in love. It did not seem to cross his mind that this relationship might be doomed, her still so young and troubled. He was a man driven by romantic notions.

In September of 1979, my dad wrote home to announce that my mom "is a very well-cultured, outgoing, artistic human being. We complement each other well and happen to be very much in love. We are engaged but haven't set a date yet. You're going to love her. She is a dream."

My grandma Emma told me that my dad was a different person after he joined the Army. Not because of the institution itself, but because that's around the time he started to heavily use drugs. It was the '70s, and many experimented with marijuana and acid, but my grandma Emma said my dad changed from the sweet man he once was and became distant and disengaged with the family. She suspected he was forced out of the Army after they found marijuana in his locker. He claimed he was only holding it for a friend, and she never pushed him on the matter.

It was during this time that my mom met my dad in Germany. I could tell that my dad was trying hard to impress his father with his newfound motivation in life. He talked of plans to leverage his VA loans to kickstart a business venture and wanted to build a cabin on the family property. "I know this isn't everything," he said, "but if we take a little at a time, eventually everything will get taken care of. Thank you, Dad, for your interest, love, and support."

My dad included a note for my grandma at the end: "Mom, I didn't mean to [not include] you but mostly I'm responding to Dad's letter (men talk you know). I'm thinking about you." His excitement overshadowed their strained communications but his exclusion of directly sharing the news of his new love feels out of character from the caring young man he used to be towards her.

My grandpa Lorenzo and Mom returned to Virginia as my dad's enlistment came to an end. My dad made plans to drive to Virginia to pick up my mom and take her to Ohio, where they would begin their life together. By this time, I was a tiny nugget in my mom's womb and preparations for their wedding were underway.

My parents embodied the essence of the '70s with their unruly hair, hippie clothes, and tan, wiry bodies. The future seemed full of promise. My dad now aspired to be a writer and work in the medical field. My mom, who had always excelled in math, would end up joining the Coast Guard to pursue engineering. I often wonder if she had other dreams before marriage and motherhood changed the trajectory of her life. Or was her main goal to escape her father, and any path away from him was welcome?

My parents were married by a justice of the peace on February 29, a leap year. A small reception was held in G.A.R. Hall, a historic meeting place for the Grand Army of the Republic and social gatherings dating back to the late 1880s for social activism and historical events. A fitting choice for the times.

In the wedding pictures, my mom looked stunning in a dress that her mom had made for her. It was floor length with delicate lace sleeves. The veil attached to a white sun hat. She clutched a handful of pink and white daisies and her slight baby bump showed when she turned to the side.

My dad wore a black tuxedo, an oversized bow tie, and a neatly trimmed mustache. His grin was almost as big as his hair as he lightly put his hand on my mom's back as they entered the building.

The wedding was small and had minimal attendance. At the reception, a three-tier wedding cake sat on a table in the front, the plastic bride and groom looking happy and hopeful. A few tables were neatly set, and people mingled and took pictures as they waited for dinner to be served. The event wrapped up quickly and they were soon off to start their new life together.

5

A year after I was born, my mom decided she wanted to join the workforce. My dad would take care of me and go back to school. It suited him, as he still struggled to identify a career for himself. And he would be with his baby girl, whom he loved very much. But the plan wasn't that simple, and he soon found himself in a cat-and-mouse game with his wife. She chose to join the Coast Guard, which while admirable, seemed to give her the opportunity to escape domestic life. At nineteen, she took off for basic training in New Jersey.

As if Dad was the paparazzi and Mom a famous actress, he followed her from city to city. He would be told *No Visitors* while she was in Coast Guard training and then suddenly, she was off to another location. First, we moved to Massachusetts, and then Maine a few months later, but we couldn't seem to catch her. In love and lonely, Dad would call but her phone would only ring and ring. She didn't even have the mercy of an answering machine to pick up.

Despite the chase, we liked living in Maine. Dad found a group of friends and I was the wild child running around, all smiles. One of my dad's friends brought over a dollhouse for me. It was plain but functional, the water ran in the sink and the toilet flushed. The delicate furniture was small, even in my young hands. It was precious and I wanted to protect it. I channeled all my energy toward not being clumsy, a trait that started rearing its ugly head.

One day, I decided to play a game which consisted of me running out the side door and then back in through the front door. I was going in fast circles and laughing the whole time, until I tripped on the sill of the doorframe and came crashing down, eyelid making contact with a rusty door hinge. I was rushed to the ER, where they put a patch over my injured eye. I looked like a pirate. To this day, I have a Frankenstein-like scar under the arch of my left eyebrow, a few centimeters from my eyeball. This was one of many visible reminders of my messy life to come.

We stayed in Maine for a couple of years, hovering near my mom's orbit. One day my dad heard from her. She was going to get an abortion. He set the receiver down and put his head in his hands. He would drive her there. But as they drove, he broke the silence and begged her to keep the baby. I was two years old and needed a sibling. He would care for this baby, providing enough love for the both. Maybe he thought this anchor would finally keep her in one place. But she was a speedboat and we as light as acorns.

My sister, Jill, was born in the spring of 1983. By Thanksgiving, Mom had already left for New York to attend electronic specialist school. She was twenty-one, showing high aptitude for math and science, and no longer the shy girl my dad had met. In fact, she hadn't been for quite some time, we would come to find out. Men found her desirable and she understood the power she held over them. She was having a string of affairs.

When she came home for two short days over Christmas, Dad suggested she take me to the store. I looked at her shyly and heard her say, "I need alone time." She walked out the front door, the frosty air that washed in somehow warmer than her presence.

Mom would only come to see us a couple of times over the next six months. She was reassigned to Chesapeake, VA, and we followed her one last time. Dad had a deep well of love for her, lowering the bucket again and again. But soon it would come back up, filled with mud and little stones. This love that felt like sludge.

I was almost four years old and had just learned how to do cartwheels. I was sure my dad would be beside himself with excitement to watch me. After calling his name several times, I realized he wasn't listening. I sat down quietly in the middle of the living room, wanting to be polite…but also noticed.

Sunlight streamed through the windows. Like a dreamy figure of a man, Dad brushed past me, his short locks alight from the rays. He paced between the kitchen and a bedroom in the back of the house, squeezing milk on his wrist to test the warmth. He had a baby to take care of and my mom was nowhere to be found. Distracted and exhausted, he stepped right over me.

Sometime later, I was excited. Mom was coming home. I ran at breakneck speed to see her, but I tripped on a crack in the sidewalk and fell hard on my right knee. Blood ran freely down my leg and into my sneaker. It didn't hurt much though and I did a hop, skip, drag combination home.

I saw the repulsed look on her face. She put a couple of Band-Aids over a cut that needed stitches. It took a long time for the cut to heal. It probably didn't help that I picked at it constantly.

The new year of 1985 brought new secrets to the surface. Dad found out that Mom had an abortion about a year earlier, during one of the long spells of not seeing her, so he knew it was not his. She admitted to having affairs with men while in New York, of which she could not deny because love letters were showing up to the house. This still did not break the camel's back.

Over the next six months, Mom was around more but she was drinking at home or going to bars quite frequently. She would pick us up from daycare visibly buzzed, if she remembered to pick us up at all. One day, she burned the back of my sister's hand with an iron. Not on accident. She tried to say Jill knocked it over and burned herself. But the scar on my sister's hand looked deliberate, the lines sharp, like when someone uses an iron to make a grilled cheese sandwich in a comedy movie. I am not sure if it was alcohol induced, her mean streak surfacing, or both. My dad still stood by her side.

He stayed until she left us a couple of months later, my fifth birthday right around the corner. She left so quietly this time, offering no breadcrumbs to follow. So, we packed up our meager belongings and headed back to the place I had been born.

6

When my parents were young, unemployed, and had a child on the way, my grandma Emma welcomed them into the homestead, the house always brimming with activity. My parents lived in the utility room off the kitchen. Mom, who was getting more swollen each day, did not complain about the tiny space and the damp that seeped through from the summer rains. My grandma Emma was kind and cooked meals for the family, kept the home clean, and was always welcoming. Despite the small utility room, Mom could move freely through the house and outside to the large property. She was not being watched, and for the first time she could breathe. Her polite gratitude would not last very long however.

My parents needed more space with my impending arrival, so my uncle Jeff helped them fix up the summer house. It was a simple structure to the left of the main house and next to the pool. Eventually there was running water and electricity thanks to some clever wiring connecting to the main house. It was not quite the cabin my dad imagined building, but it was rustic, simple, and fit well with their desire of living off the grid. And between the summer and the main house was a large piece of land where they would plant a garden. They tended to it for a short time, but it was quickly taken over and became unruly. Later, my sister and I would randomly find root vegetables and bring them to grandma Emma for her stews.

Inside the summer house, the floors were unfinished and covered in a mix of gifted furnishings. In the living room was an iron fireplace with an orange shag rug in front. Spots of soot blended in its fibers and my parents would rest me in front of the warm flames, tucked into my baby rocker. To the left was my future crib, a ducky baby blanket slung over its side, and a couple of stuffed animals resting on the mattress. An Oriental rug lay alongside the shag, the contrast of decorations striking.

They had moved in a rocking chair and a highchair in preparation for me. One of my grandma Emma's knitted quilts was folded into a makeshift cushion for the many nights I would need to be gently rocked to sleep. A quilt that my dad would get to know well.

A chair and pillows from my grandma Grace looked fancy next to the bookshelf overflowing with books, piles of wood for the fire, and the desk covered in papers, a typewriter, papers, and a few beer bottles. She had also gifted a beautiful, yellow silk comforter covered in butterflies. It sparkled in my parents' small bedroom against the dark walls and furniture.

It was late one August night when my mom went into labor. We were miles of dark windy roads away from the hospital and I was coming fast. My dad had a bit of medical experience from his time in the Army and had been preparing for the moment. They were ready to bring me into the world in that summer house.

My mom was calm as her water broke. She looked at my dad and said, "It's time."

He smiled and said, "I'll be right back."

My dad crossed through the then budding garden to the main house. The moon shone bright overhead and the buzz of insects was loud and insistent. He opened the front door and my uncle Jeff and grandma Emma looked up from their conversation.

"The baby is coming!" my dad said. Everyone's faces lit up as they set drinks down and moved toward the door.

It was hot in the summer house. The windows were open, and a light breeze swirled the smells of summer, sweat, and birth together. My mom was on her back, her body tense and ready to deliver me, naturally. Dad held her legs as he coached her breathing and pushing. This would be painful, but she had youth and determination on her side.

My grandma Emma was eager to meet me as she paced the length of the small room. My uncle stood by my dad and took a flurry of Polaroid pictures as I began my ascent into their lives. They would create a photo album of this experience that I would see later, one of the few pieces of evidence that my mom and I were connected. I knew that at least once, she felt something real between us, even if it was the physical pain and exhilaration of delivering me.

Everyone was surprised when my dad declared that I was a girl. They all thought I was going to be a boy based on an old wives' tale of a low hanging belly. They planned to name me Michael and were suddenly at a loss for a girl's name. A few days later, when they registered me with the county they said, "Her name is

Persephone Grey." The clerk asked about my middle name and my mom said, "She can pick one out when she gets older." But I never did.

My dad cradled me in his hands and cut my umbilical cord. He handed me to my grandma Emma, and she brought me over to the large metal wash basin in the kitchen. She bathed and dressed me, her first granddaughter, before she reluctantly handed me to my mom.

"You were so tiny and beautiful," my grandma Emma told me years later. She wanted to keep holding me safely against her warm chest. Something was off with my mom, a slight detachment that was discernible amongst the excitement. But my grandma Emma had handed me over, beginning the realization for my mom that she did not know what to do with me. She couldn't bring herself to make eye contact. She did not know to hold me close to her heart so I could feel the comfort of her heartbeat. My cries and coos would confuse her as she tried to understand what I needed.

Over the next several months, she would go through the motions. My mom would wrap a blanket around her waist and tuck me into the back as she did chores. My dad captured a moment when

36

she was trying to breastfeed me, the rocking chair pulled up close to the iron fireplace. I clutch these worn Polaroid pictures; I listen hard as if I might be able to hear her speaking to the tiny baby in her arms. I try to make her say, "I love you, sweet girl."

From those early years, my grandma Emma saved a handful of letters, poetry, stories, and artwork from my parents. They were always leaving something behind as we moved in and out of the property. Grandma Emma would add the items to a box in the barn she kept for them, thinking they might want to reclaim their items at some point. But the box collected dust and mildew for decades, until she stumbled upon it in her garage. She had brought it with her from Ohio to Florida, after she sold the family property. She had always wanted to return these items to their rightful owner, and she then realized that the rightful owner was me.

This box of memories would help me piece together secrets and timelines that had been withheld from me my whole life. These contents humanized my parents, acting as a surrogate for them by answering questions that nobody else seemed willing or able to answer.

Sometimes I breathe in the musty smell of the paper, trying to imprint who they were. I try to weave in my impressions of their imagination, confessions, and experiences. I fill in the gaps so I can tell myself the stories they never told me. I wonder what it would have been like to talk about life, art, and poetry with this version of them. Or any version of them.

7

The best times of my childhood were spent at the homestead in Ohio. The main house rested at the top of a large hill. From the road, a long, gravel driveway snaked up for what seemed to be two miles. Running parallel, on the right side, was a creek, and at the halfway point, it fed in and out of a large pond brimming with activity. Frogs jumped across the lily pads as water moccasins glided past. Dragonflies and mosquitoes danced on the surface, wings glittery and light. Cattails grew along the border and were soft to the touch. Woods hugged the pond's perimeter and when the sun passed through the trees, the water would filter the rays like a prism.

In the winter, the pond would freeze over and turn into a makeshift ice-skating rink. Lacking ice skates, the kids renamed the sport "boot skating" and would race across the pond, laughing and pulling each other down as we spun out of control. There was a mini hill between the pond and driveway, which we nicknamed the "fun hill" and would sled there for hours. It was steep and death-defying, and it's a wonder nobody was ever injured.

At this halfway point, there was a barn to the left where we kept chickens, rabbits, and even a horse. The surrounding fields were filled with tall grass and wildflowers in the spring. When the wind blew, the movement of the grass gave the sensation of watching the tide wash in and out. Honeysuckle grew in abundance and we would carefully pull the stems out of the flower and lick the nectar.

I had loved our horse, Mo. I wasn't sure where he had come from, but one day I found him living in the barn. I didn't question this new addition; my grandma Emma's house always had people coming and going and it was no different for animals. A horse showing up was no big deal.

My dad taught me how to bathe and brush Mo after a long day of grazing the fields. I would feed him apples and sugar cubes, and watch him chew and blink his eyes, the lashes moving slowly as if in a deep daydream. He was gentle and sweet, and he took a liking to me.

One day, I asked my dad to teach me to ride. Mo wasn't very tall, and my dad picked me up and placed me on his back. He showed me how to properly sit, how to direct with my bare heels, which commands to use to go faster, slower, and to stop. I didn't know most people used saddles. I rode bareback, my fingers twisted gently into Mo's thick mane.

We didn't have a fence along our property line, and Mo used to wander onto the neighbor's property. Sometimes he'd be gone for days. We left Ohio during one of his breaks; I never got to say goodbye.

On the edge of the fields grew thick blackberry bushes. Generations of children would pick berries for Grandma Emma to make delicious pies. For hours, we combed past pricklers and areas where the bees had staked claim to find the perfect berries. Buckets would fill up as we feasted on the too squishy or under-ripe ones, the taste of sunshine warm in our mouths.

The driveway led up to the house and circled toward a large tree in the front. As cars pulled up and engines rumbled to a stop, you could hear the dogs bark in both greeting and warning. Cats would lazily raise their heads to assess the situation and children might shout hellos depending on who was visiting or living there at the time.

Steps led up to a large front porch. A globe hung within an iron chandelier from the porch ceiling, providing a soft glow day or night. An ornate side table was flanked by two red leather chairs and a wicker couch was tucked to the right. Mismatched wood chairs faced toward them making a semicircle—the scene set for many long days and nights filled with philosophical conversation and reflection.

The front door opened into a foyer and the kitchen was straight ahead. Off the kitchen was a utility room where my parents used to sleep. There was a backdoor, and it doubled as a storage room. To the right was a loft-style living room with a fireplace which provided warmth during the winter days. Large windows in the front living room made the outside world look like a moving painting.

The walls and floors were a dark wood and on sunny days, the bright light brought a soft amber glow into the rooms. During the winter, we sat in stark contrast to the white snow piled against the windows and spread across the landscape as far as one could see. On especially snowy days, it looked like someone had painted the windows white, and blank eyes stared at us as we scooted closer to the fireplace for warmth.

To the right of the fireplace was a short hallway leading to the back right quadrant of the house. Here was the only bathroom and my grandparents' bedroom. A chair was in the bathroom so the adults could supervise our baths during the times they could finally get us in there. We were wild children and preferred a dip in the pond to a warm bath.

There was a door on the right wall of the living room that led to the "up for grabs" room. We all took turns staking claim, as we moved in and out. Stairs led up to the attic from here and the small room was guarded by a door requiring a turn from a skeleton key. Books, toys, and blankets were stacked in the corners, waiting for us at night and on bad weather days. A tiny door on the left side of the room opened to a ledge overlooking the living room. We loved to crawl on that ledge and spy on the adults when we thought they weren't paying attention. On especially daring days, when we were sure no adults were around, we would jump onto the couch below.

The summer house fell into disarray after my parents moved out and the pool had long been left to the elements, filled with all the scraps and debris one would expect to find in a junkyard. We would treat that pool like a playground, dodging sharp edges and pockets of air between the piles of junk. As we raced across the length of the

pool, we would narrowly avoid stepping on tiny snake heads that

popped up searching for the source of vibrations.

8

When we moved back to Ohio in 1985, I was entering kindergarten and began to blossom now that we were in a more stabilized environment. I was growing up and learning life skills, like how to tie my shoes. I loved going to school and I joined the Brownies. We did cool stuff, like science experiments and camping. I was a curious child with a love for nature and creativity.

I excelled in school, especially math, and I apparently loved to be the center of attention. On my kindergarten school record, it says "[Persephone] has a tendency to want to be the center of attention. Sometimes she has difficulty sharing with peers." I have a picture from a play we did in school. I am standing in the middle, hamming it up with a deep curtsy and a bright smile.

My favorite pastime was hanging out with my extended family. Grandma Emma was sweet and loving, I had cousins my age, and an aunt who was only a few years older than me. We ruled the property and spent hours playing outside. We would catch tiny, grey crayfish in the creeks which ran through our property. The icy water would numb our feet and hands as we dug under rocks in search of our temporary pets. I would collect snakes and place them in a bucket.

I loved the woods and the fields. We would explore the woods in increments of time which would result in an AMBER alert today. We camped in the front yard, played badminton, and stole fresh ears of corn from the neighboring fields. Way back in the woods my cousins and I found what looked like gravestones and a big wooden cross. In the house, almost every member of my family would see a ghost, have terrible nightmares, and feel like they were being watched.

We would swim and catch frogs and tadpoles. Sometimes my dad would boil frog's legs and add Cajun spice. We would pretend we were giants eating chicken wings. I would take the skin he peeled from the frog legs and put them on my fingers and chase my sister around like I was a frog monster out to capture her.

We would go roller skating quite a bit. I even took lessons and learned how to roller skate backwards. I was a limbo champ. We would buy huge Pixy Stix and get high off the powdered candy. The sensation of the disco lights, the sugar coating my tongue, and the excitement of being with friends spin around my head in slow motion. I want to lock fingers with this memory as friends would lock fingers as they spun around and around the rink.

The first dog I ever loved was named Cleo and she would follow me everywhere... or maybe it was me following her. She went missing one day and I eventually found her old, lifeless body in our favorite hiding place where several bushes grew together in a circle. The place where we cuddled and played for so many afternoons, our private room in the woods.

Our house was lively and often there were bonfires with lots of loud, young friends of my uncles and Dad. Motorcycles were everywhere and the air was thick with beer foam, roasting meat, and a tense excitement.

Motorcycles were always around. One time I was trying to be cool and I climbed atop a mountain of a bike. I wore a two-piece bathing suit, no doubt planning on swimming in one of our many ponds. The bike was a work in progress and there was a sharp piece of metal jutting out. It sliced deep into my left hip, leaving a visible scar which has never faded.

I have a Mead notebook that my grandma Emma managed to save for me. I made this sometime between 1985 to 1989, before I knew how to spell "poem" correctly. It's titled "Peom Book." There are a series of my favorite poems.

My mom only visited us a handful of times over these idyllic years, which made what happened next even more shocking.

9

It was the summer of 1989, right before my ninth birthday. I sat next to my sister on the front porch as we watched Mom walk up our long driveway with a man. The bright summer sun made the red Toyota Celica at the end of the driveway sparkle like a cherry-colored disco ball. I scratched at the mosquito bites on my legs.

I glanced at Dad, his siblings, and grandma Emma, who all instinctively moved to form a protective shield around me and my sister. The sound of our dogs' half-greeting/half-warning barks cut through the air as my dad broke formation to stop the unwelcome visitors from getting any closer. After a few moments of muted conversation, Mom and the man abruptly turned around and made their way back to the car, the angry crunch of their steps echoing as they left.

My dad was on edge. Mom had called me a few days earlier to say, "I want you to come live with me. You can have your own bedroom and we have a pool that you can swim in."

I looked out our kitchen window to the summer house, where I had been born, all of it long left to the elements. Weeds and flowers poked through rotted planks of wood. The hinges were rusted, and the windows cracked. This tiny place where I had made my entrance into the world resembled a haunted house, but in my mind, it was beautiful.

I liked our pool filled with junk. My cousins and I would sort through the broken objects tossed in there and create something new. We'd tuck away into tiny spaces while playing hide-and-seek. We didn't need our pool to be filled with water; we had ponds and a creek that ran through the property, and small waterfalls, easily reached by a short hike into the woods behind our house. Besides, there was a pool at the Holiday Inn where grandma Emma took us some weekends. We'd swim until the chlorine nearly blinded us and our fingers pruned.

As far as my own bedroom, that was the last thing I wanted. I always shared a room with my sister and cousins. Always had someone to giggle with as we fought sleep and terrors of monsters under our beds.

More importantly, this woman was a stranger, and I loved my dad.

"No, thank you," I told her. I didn't trust her, and I certainly wasn't going anywhere with someone I only really knew from pictures.

A few days after my mom's visit and much discussion among the adults, my sister and I found ourselves taking stock of our belongings. We had been down this road before. We were told to pack an overnight bag, but we knew we needed to be sure to bring our most prized possessions, lest we lose them forever.

We lined our toys side by side to evaluate which would come with us and which would be left behind. Mr. Bear, my favorite stuffed animal and nightly cuddle buddy since I was six, was my first choice. My Cabbage Patch doll and Popples came next. I'd started to have anxiety-ridden dreams. I needed a backup cuddle option.

After a tough debate, I tucked my Prince Charles and Princess Diana dolls into my bag as well. They were so dignified—

him with his full military outfit and her with a sparkly silver dress and a sheer cape lined with soft, white feathers. I wasn't sure why I liked them so much, but this well-dressed couple felt like something special to hang onto.

I happily left my Barbie dolls behind, still in their boxes. I actively disliked them, maybe because they were from my mean grandpa Lorenzo or because Barbie didn't fit into my idea of playtime. One of the adults once dressed me up in a kid-sized Cinderella dress and I had wandered down to the pond in it. After a couple of hours, I came back to the house with a bucket full of snakes, covered head to toe in mud. I wasn't in trouble but grandma Emma half-smiled as she advised me that this was not how a girl in a dress should play. I didn't stop wearing dresses though; we wore whatever hand-me-downs were given to us. But I didn't stop playing in the mud or collecting snakes either. Amongst my family, I didn't have to be like all the other little girls.

Realizing I had to leave my other toys behind, my heart squeezed a little, but there was no more room left in my tiny backpack. I peeked at my sister's pile to see if maybe I could fit more of my things into her bag but her own face was creased with concern.

Dad kept our goodbyes to the family light. After all, we were just going to stay one town over with our longtime babysitter, Shelly. We would see our family again, real soon. Or so we all thought.

10

Our babysitter, Shelly, lived in the suburbs, where houses were only a few steps apart and lawns were littered with toys and patio furniture. Neighborhood children rode bikes on the street and played in yards. There weren't any fields or ponds to explore but we made do with the century-old graveyard to the left of her house.

Now, during the day, we weren't permitted to play outside. We understood that we were hiding from Mom and because we loved Dad so much, we allowed ourselves to be locked inside, away from the bright summer sunshine we so craved.

The inside of Shelly's home was welcoming but dirty. We spent our days sitting on the saggy old couch, with the hum of the filter a large fish tank's filter buzzing in our ears. There was a tiny treasure chest inside the tank, and even though I knew it was fake, I wanted to reach in and claim the tiny little gold coins and jewels for my very own. Algae crept up all four sides of the glass despite the sucker fish methodically working their way across its surface day and night. The other fish looked fragmented and pale green beneath the overhead lights.

When Dad was there, he'd peek through the closed blinds as my sister and I stayed out of view. We started sitting still and learned how to be quiet, as if Mom had binoculars, ready to peer in as soon as the curtain slipped open. As if she had a drinking glass, her ear pressed against one end and the house pressed against the other.

Shelly watched other kids too, including my best friend, Emily. It helped ease the loneliness to have her around. My sister would play quietly next to us as we watched movies on the VCR. We covered her eyes and ears during scary or inappropriate scenes, although it seemed as if an adult should have been doing that for us.

As the days passed, we watched *Dirty Dancing* dozens of times. I did not understand the movie completely, but I got the gist. Together, Baby and I learned about class status, breaking the rules, and true love.

We watched *Nightmare on Elm Street*, *Porky's*, and *Mask*. I realized I had a taste for horror and drama. There were piles of VHS tapes and we kept popping them in to watch over and over. Nobody ever stopped us. I had never watched so much TV.

I could feel my innocence slipping away when we saw *Dolls* and *Child's Play*, my view forever changed of my beloved toys. I would whisper, "Goodnight, I love you," to them several times before bed each night, afraid they would kill me in my sleep if I didn't.

We nibbled on fast food with eyes glued to the television. We were fascinated by language we knew was bad and the semi-nude scenes made us fidget and giggle. When adults were present, they felt more like shadows and muffled voices in our peripheral view. I think we may have felt the same to them.

Some afternoons we sat upstairs where we could open the curtains and crack the windows. Here, we painstakingly worked on jigsaw puzzles, our sweaty foreheads furrowed in concentration as we aligned each piece accordingly. We glued the completed puzzles to poster board, let them dry for a day, then hung them on the wall with brightly colored thumbtacks. "Does it look straight?" we'd ask each other, as if we were curators decorating an art gallery.

At night we could play outside with the neighborhood kids while the adults socialized. We crossed over to the old cemetery. It was just a few steps away but felt as though we were entering another world. Trees grew tall and were spaced apart, causing the moonlight to fall in patches across the graves. The headstones were crumbling, and their etchings were barely visible.

I liked to run my fingers down the smooth granite, finding the cracks filled with weeds and tiny flowers. The tips of my fingers lingered on the petals as I tried to set the colors in my mind, to remember what they looked like when we were locked away in the daylight.

We'd sing, "The worms crawl in, the worms crawl out," as the handful of us got ready to play hide-and-seek. Us older kids would hide and make the younger ones count to fifty before trying to find us. They usually only made it to fifteen or twenty, so we knew we had to hide quickly behind large tree trunks and gravestones. We didn't really care about them finding us. The real fun was to scare them. As a seeker passed, we'd grab their ankles and groan like zombies craving brains.

They'd get so scared that they'd burst into tears, which then made us cry. Sniffling, we'd wander back to the house where the adults sat on the porch, smoking cigarettes and drinking. The electric fly zapper was somehow calming as it sizzled and crackled, the blue light shimmering and running waves across our faces after each pop.

Some nights, we'd tuck Mason jars under our arms and chase the endless fireflies. We'd catch them in the jars, pinching off some of their butts to rub their iridescence on our arms, so we too could glow.

11

Then one night, we suddenly packed our stuff and left for Maine. My sister and I felt scared and confused as my dad put hundreds of miles between what had safely felt like a second home and this unknown new destination. We didn't ask Dad questions, just put on our brave faces for yet another adventure.

At first, we stayed with a blond-haired woman in a very old house. While she was nice, it didn't seem like she was excited to have us there. We weren't allowed to flush toilet paper down the toilet. She made sure to tell us that many times. Feeling uneasy, we tiptoed across the creaky floors with a politeness not usually reserved for children. I held my sister's hand issuing a *"Shhhh"* quietly under my breath.

I started fourth grade, and having no friends at our new school, sat alone at lunch. One day, they served sandwiches. Noticing the lack of meat and cheese poking out of the sides, I pried the slices of bread apart. I saw peanut butter and a gooey white cream, which after a quick taste, I realized was marshmallow. I thought about how I roasted marshmallows over campfires and pictured the cafeteria ladies in the back warming up marshmallows, pulling the burnt pieces off the outside, and spreading the melted insides onto our sandwiches.

Everyone was calmly eating their sandwiches, but it felt like dessert for lunch. I ate mine quickly, excited that it wasn't bologna and cheddar, but irrationally thinking it could metamorphosis into that at any moment. Maybe this place wasn't so bad after all.

I loved art class. One day, we were given crayons and drawing paper. My teacher told us to close our eyes and to start drawing a shape until she said to stop. From there, we were told to come up with a story. When I opened my eyes, I saw a large blob with some fin-like shapes skirting its edges. I decided my shape was a fish and set about adding eyes, big red lips, stripes, and lots of bright colors.

I now had the inspiration for my story and began to create characters and a plot line. I thought, *where does my fish live?* Instantly, I pictured him swimming in a moat. I also saw two dragons and a castle. I thought about the king who lived inside and how much the dragons loved him.

I drew the dragons and wrote a chapter for each one. The first dragon, Zaggy, was responsible for keeping the king happy, but he had anxiety because everyone made fun of his two tails. He ended up locking himself in his room because he became convinced, he would trip over one of his tails and hurt the king.

The other dragon, Purple Zex, lived in the moat and was responsible for protecting the castle. He loved his job and never wanted to leave, but he too was unhappy. He had droopy ears and was teased endlessly for them. He only came out at night when nobody could see him.

I started to draw the castle, with fish swimming in the moat. But I didn't get to finish my story because we were moving again. It had only been a couple of months and I was devastated to have to leave. For someone who was only nine years old, I was beginning to collect too many moments of unfinished business, of rushed departures, of not being able to say goodbye.

As we drove to our next location, I imagined that Zaggy and Purple Zex were going to become best friends with the fish. They would all be one happy family of misfits who protected the castle together. The king would realize how much they loved him and order all the bullies out of his kingdom so the dragons would never have to hide again.

12

In late October, we moved to our own, small house in Maine. Dad had gotten a job at a local radio station and he worked out a deal with his new employer for this bare-boned structure. The house was right next to a tall radio tower and was likely meant for one single person to live in, not a man and his two young daughters.

Dad's new job was only two miles from our new home and school. I took care of myself and my sister after school until he returned in the evenings, and I knew he worried about leaving us alone. A cat we named Patches decided to adopt us and somehow this furry babysitter made us all feel better.

Winter broke and despite having lived through many snowstorms in Ohio, we'd never seen anything like winter in Maine. The natural piles went well above my head and the snow was heavy, not powdery. My dad, always able to create fun and adventure, suggested we carve out tunnels using pots and pans. My sister and I giggled as we scooped snow out and threw it behind us, my dad using a shovel to make real progress. After digging out a short tunnel, we started to carve out an igloo we could all fit into, including Patches, who would snuggle in with us as we made up stories and laughed to keep warm.

We were making the best of our situation even though we were scared. Every moment my sister and I were alone without my dad, I would imagine Mom or the police showing up to take us away from him. I was young but I knew we were on the run, and probably in trouble. I could tell that Dad was upset as he spoke in hushed tones to family members and his lawyer back in Ohio. Worry lines creased his forehead and a deep pain suddenly darkened his eyes. He looked at us like we could disappear at any moment. Each time he hugged us, his gentle arms now a steel cage.

The dynamics of our lives had changed. I felt like I had to be different, more mature, more responsible. When Dad wasn't around, someone had to take on the role of "adult." Little kids played games and did homework. They didn't make dinner and monitor homework and make sure everyone was bathed.

My dad had been taking care of us without my mom for years, but we always had other adults around. Here we were completely isolated. He was doing the best he could, but he couldn't be there all the time. I had to help.

I learned how to ignite a pilot light and could warm up dinner. I made sure we did our homework and the house was tidy. My sister looked to me to keep her safe. I went from playmate to mom figure, even though I could barely see over the counter. I learned how to use a phone book as a stepping stool as I cooked on the stove.

My sister began to cling to me like I clung to Mr. Bear. I stopped carrying him around to make room for her in my arms. I kept him tucked under my covers, head on my pillow, until I crawled into bed. Exhausted and anxious, it was my turn to cling.

The days were short, and the winter brought on fierce storms. One early evening, before my dad was home and as the sun was setting, the wind knocked the electricity out. This was too big for me to handle. The small house suddenly became a mansion of expanding dark rooms and hallways. Winds pushed hard against the house, rattling the windows and shaking icicles from the gutters.

There was little visibility as I peered outside, wishing for the headlights of Dad's car to appear. He would know how to bring the electricity back.

I rustled around the kitchen cabinets and found half a candle and one match. My little fingers were cold but luckily the match struck on the first try. I lit the candle and the pilot light in the gas stove to give us a little warmth. My sister and I huddled close to the flickering candlelight, trying to get away from the dark shadows behind us. Somewhere in the room, Patches meowed quietly.

As the minutes dragged on and we sat in silence, I tried to think of ways to make this a fun adventure. Like Dad was always able to do. I decided to pretend to blow the candle out to entertain us. At least it was something to do. Or maybe I had watched too many horror movies and it had brought out my dark side. Or maybe the only way I thought to not be scared was to try to control what was scaring me. *So what* if the candle went out? I could handle it.

My sister laughed nervously as I kept on the charade. But my breath accidently slipped through my partially pursed lips and as the flame died out, we clutched each other. I said, "Okay, just close your eyes for a minute and then open them. We'll see better after that."

We took a few breaths and opened our eyes, adjusting to the dark. We still had the warmth from the gas stove and Patches, sensing our distress, lay in our laps.

Dad came home to find us cuddled together in the dark telling each other stories. I felt an instant relief; the stress drained out of my body. We didn't tell him about the candle. It felt like that moment belonged to us, a secret for us to share. After getting the electricity back on, he gave us a long hug.

We had survived this storm and with the terror drowned out by the light and Dad's presence I thought, *I handled it okay after all.* This experience has stayed with me. I realized that things could turn out okay if I did mess up, but then I also gave fuel to my growing anxieties. I began playing *what if* scenarios in my head, over and over.

13

At Christmas time, we had a small tree in the living room with a scattering of presents underneath. My sister and I woke up very early that morning and decided to open our presents. I don't know if we were acting out or just excited. Maybe it was a combination of both. Or I was feeling like a decision maker, having taken on more responsibility. We had never opened presents without adults around before, but I greenlighted the idea. I could have felt like we deserved it, getting a few toys after having abandoned so many. It didn't cross my mind that Dad might get upset about us opening our presents without him.

I turned a package over in my hands. The wrapping paper looked the same as other presents from grandma Emma and a thought crept into my head. I looked at the tag and could tell that it was stacked on top of another. I was peeling back the "From: Santa" sticker to reveal a "From: Grandma" sticker when my dad came into the living room and caught us surrounded by flimsy paper boxes, tissue paper, and trinkets.

His voice cracked as he asked, "What are you girls doing?" The crestfallen look on his face was so heartbreaking, I still feel a deep shame for taking that moment from him. Sharing Christmas morning and seeing the joy on our faces would have been jet fuel for his soul. But we had ruined it.

I smoothed the tag back down, quickly processing and filing away that Santa was not real. I was more upset that my dad was sad. We apologized as we hugged him and attempted to salvage the day by gathering the remaining unopened presents to open with him.

If I had known that would be the last Christmas we'd spend together, I would have slept in later, not opened a single present without him. I would have made Dad breakfast and snuggled with him all day. I would have thrown his keys deep into the piles of snow, so we could never drive back to Ohio. But I didn't know any of these things at the time.

14

A couple of weeks later, my dad made the decision to go back to Ohio. At the time, I thought this meant everything was going to be okay. But I found out years later that his lawyer told him there was a warrant out for his arrest. He'd missed a custody hearing and had technically kidnapped us by taking us out of state. He was told it would be best to come back to Ohio to deal with the situation, otherwise the consequences would get substantially worse. His lawyer led him to believe that he had a strong case for keeping custody of us if he returned immediately.

We packed our belongings into a hard-plastic cargo trunk, boxes, and garbage bags. Dad seemed to be in a hurry, moving too fast as he loaded the car and strapped the cargo trunk to the roof. I clutched Mr. Bear, no longer feeling responsible or strong. I couldn't find Patches and a new emotion was sweeping over me. Panic.

Patches was an outdoor cat but didn't stay out for long as it was the dead of winter. "Patches! Patches!" I shouted. The banks of snow absorbed the sound of my calls, my throat closing up against the frigid winter air. Eventually Dad said it was time to go. For a moment, I stood my ground and refused to get into the car. I fought with him for the first time I could remember.

"Dad! Patches is going to freeze to death! She is going to starve to death!" I kept saying this over and over. What I didn't say was that Patches would be sad that we abandoned her. That even if she survived, she would never forgive us betraying her trust when we were supposed to love her.

Dad swore he tried to find her but assured me that she was a smart cat and would be fine. He picked me up and put me in the back of the car. I could have kicked and screamed but my heart was aching, and it seemed to drain the energy from my tiny body. I vividly remember thinking; *I will never forgive you for this.*

I stared out of the window for miles in case Patches suddenly bounded out of the woods toward our car. I sent her psychic messages of apology, repeating it over and over in my head as my heart squeezed tight. But I didn't cry. Brave face on, I didn't shed one tear.

We raced down the highway, back to Ohio. The buzz of the engine had almost lulled me to sleep when I heard a snapping sound. The truck pulled slightly from side to side as the wind swept the lid off the cargo trunk strapped to the roof of the car. I turned to watch, helpless, as my things flew out.

For the second time that day, I raised my voice at him. "DAD! The trunk is open! My toys are falling out everywhere! Please stop!" But whatever had possessed him to take off so quickly we had to leave our cat behind was still there, a mysterious force placing thick palms over his ears so he could not hear me. His gaze never left the road ahead of him. My sister, sitting in the front seat, was silent except for the intermittent sniffles she couldn't suppress.

Feeling numb, I shrank back into the seat. I said a silent goodbye to my Prince Charles and Princess Diana dolls, to my Popple with her babies in her pouch, and my Cabbage Patch doll—the toys I had chosen over all the others when we left our home with grandma Emma. I thought about that movie *Dolls* and hoped they wouldn't come alive and find me one day, angry that I had abandoned them. *I love you*, I whispered fiercely under my breath as they fell out of sight. All I could do then was curl into a ball and drift off into an exhausted, dreamless sleep.

Patches was gone and my already sparse childhood belongings had dwindled down to Mr. Bear, the clothes on my back, and the unfinished homework in my backpack. I felt a physical pain from the loss of my other things, and I resolved to cling fiercely onto what I had left.

With these losses, I imagine the seed was planted for what would become a hoarding issue as I got older. I would hold onto everything because I couldn't bear the thought of losing anything else. My things became a part of me, and to part with even the smallest object felt like a departure from myself. To throw away even a rubber band brought back the panic of seeing my clothes and toys scattered onto that snowy Maine road. Letting go of anything brought back the bitter rage of being betrayed by my dad, of the chaotic uncertainty of speeding back to Ohio. It broke me in places that were still trying to grow.

15

Back in Ohio, we stayed in a house at Avon Lake. Our babysitter Shelly helped us find the place and we enrolled in our third school for the year. We could walk to school and Dad was home much more. It felt safer here, being close to our family again. I tried to move on from Patches and the loss of my things, pretending that hadn't happened to us. That it was just another story we'd watched on a VHS tape. This also started a new pattern for me, a pattern of detaching from overwhelming moments in my life and mentally packaging these painful stories into imaginary spaces. These were someone else's stories; I just watched the tape.

The next few weeks went by quickly. We didn't have time to settle in or see everyone before the police showed up at our door. My sister and I were doing our homework while a show about baby animals played in the background. We were still giddy from the pudding I had made for dessert and from the game of catch we'd been playing with Dad after dinner in the living room. It seemed late for someone to be knocking, and as Dad walked toward the door, we put our pencils down and held our breath. Was our six-month game of hide-and-seek over? Had they found us?

When Dad opened the door, police officers stood there. "Sir, can we come inside?" one said, with a stern face.

My dad let them in, then sat on the couch next to us. "Girls, I'll be back in a little while," he said. "Your babysitter will be here soon to take care of you. I love you." He hugged us, his caging arms now a crushing force until the officers forced him to let go.

The police officers didn't wait for her to arrive. Instead, they left us with a neighbor, telling us that they'd left a note for her and she'd pick us up when she could. It did not seem like they cared about our well-being, or what we were witnessing happening to our dad, or being left with a stranger. The world was spinning around us, in shades of blue and red. We stood on the sidewalk as they pushed Dad into the patrol car. Our brave faces broken, we cried as they drove away.

The next day my mom and grandpa Lorenzo came to pick us up. My sister was screaming as they forced us into their car, but I was quiet, numb. It would be twelve years until we saw our dad again.

16

I went to an elementary school in Virginia for one week in 1990, my fourth school in one school year. I was the girl who showed up on a Monday and disappeared by Friday. I was dressed in TJ Maxx clothes to replace my hand-me-downs, which were either left behind or worn too thin. Clothes that I had worn exploring the woods, watching my grandma Emma cook, hugging my dad, and playing with my cousins.

I had never shopped in a large store before. The fluorescent lights were so bright, and the racks of clothes seemed to go on forever. I felt disoriented and so I hid behind the discount clothes, quiet as a mouse. I stayed there, in hiding, for what seemed to be a long time. A woman found me tucked away as she was thumbing through the rack. She looked startled and concerned, and took me to the front desk, where they paged my mom on the overhead speaker. She eventually showed up at the registers, seemingly unconcerned. She hadn't even noticed that I was missing. We finished shopping and headed home.

At my new school, the teachers must have sent a note home to parents asking them to include me on their children's valentine's card list. On Wednesday, like all the other kids, I had a paper bag on my desk filled with valentines. I did not know these people. Their kindness felt unexpected and strange. I was still unsteady and traumatized from the recent events. I was embarrassed, realizing I did not have anything for them.

In a short period of time, anxiety had become a companion who guarded me closely, quickly snatching words out of my mouth and replacing them with irrational thoughts inside my head. Thoughts like, *they are making fun of me, they hate me because I didn't get them cards*, and *If you are very still and quiet then they won't see you and make fun of you.*

I had become a quiet child. The only person I knew in my life now was my sister. Everyone and everything around us were strange and felt wrong. I kept telling myself that it was temporary, and we would go back home. I was observant and cautious. I was ready to make an escape.

We walked in a single file line down colorful hallways toward the gym. We played. We walked back to the classroom.

That's all I remember of that school. A colorful hallway, a gym, and a paper bag full of valentines.

Unbeknownst to me, I would see that school again four years and five schools later. My mom would divorce and remarry my stepdad and we would eventually end up back in the same place.

Years later, I'd become friends with classmates who remembered a girl who showed up during Valentine's Day. It was like walking into a thrift store and finding something that had been stolen from me years before. This experience, this memory truly belonged to me.

17

I tasted grits when we first arrived in Mississippi. We ate at a diner where I choked on a piece of steak. Not the kind of choking where you cough a few times but where you cannot breathe. I clutched at my throat and tried to get my mom's attention. I reached down my throat with pinched fingers in an attempt to grab it. It finally slid down, allowing me to gasp for air. The whole episode unnoticed, I pushed my steak aside and finished my grits.

The fifth school I went to in fourth grade was a private Catholic school. Along with my school uniform, I came into possession of my first bra. The nuns insisted we wear them so the boys could not see our undeveloped bodies through our white shirts during gym class. I had not been self-aware up to this point and I was embarrassed.

Despite the upheaval and chaos over the year, I was still an exceptional student. In the few months I would attend St. Paul's

School, I received a Certificate of Scholastic Achievement and a Certificate of Merit for Superior Achievement in the Fourth Grade Mathematics Contest.

I would attend my first seafood festival as part of a fundraiser for our school. I went from catching small, gray crayfish in a cold creek in Ohio to tables piled high with bright red, spicy bodies atop boiled corn and red potatoes. Used newspaper draped over picnic tables, quickly collecting cracked tails and tiny heads. I sucked the juice and brains, the ever-adventurous eater. I ate until my fingers were covered with tiny cuts and my lips were coated in Cajun spice—a taste that lasted for hours. I learned to rinse my hands with lemon juice and to shake off the slight sting.

I would learn about Mardi Gras, moon pies, brightly colored coins (which I hoarded even though they had no value), baby Jesus in a king cake, and beads. Later when we went to New Orleans for a night parade, I would see what the older girls would do to get the beads. I would hold my mother's hand tightly as we weaved through the crowded streets. Cigarettes swept past my face and the ground stuck to my sneakers. It was scary and exciting.

Our daytime trips to New Orleans consisted of beignets, gumbo, and visiting the River Walk, where we could pick a large jawbreaker. They were bigger than our fists and would often go moldy before we could finish them.

We lived in an apartment complex where I made friends. There was a swimming pool and we played kickball in the open fields. Being entrepreneurs, we attempted to sell Mardi Gras beads to neighbors and had lemonade stands. Influenced by Nancy Drew, my friend Mary and I started a detective agency and took it seriously. I still have the blue Lisa Frank pocket folder where we kept our case notes.

We had my tenth birthday party at the pool and invited my neighborhood friends. I rocked a very '90s yellow and black bathing suit with a belt. It reminded me of honeybees.

My sister had this T-shirt that read I SCREAM FOR ICE CREAM. We got such a kick out of that.

She was so excited to get a bike. It had PINK THUNDER stenciled on the frame. One day, she crashed it into a brick wall, and she was devastated. I think it took a great while to replace it.

We saw our first waterspout form and break apart over the ocean, a twister made of water. My sister next to me, her arms tucked into her oversized T-shirt, looked on in awe. The air was hot and thick.

We would sit around on hot summer days eating Kool-Aid mix from the packets and the older girls would throw out sex terms and giggle when the younger ones looked confused. When we asked why a guy "coming" was so funny, they told us to ask our parents. But we knew better.

Mary and I would collect things like tampons, candy bars, and magazines to keep in a box under her bed. When Milli Vanilli was declared a fraud, we heard that the police would be going door to door to collect their tapes. So, we hid ours in the secret box.

We loved NKOTB, especially Joey and Jonathan. We would pretend to call them and plan dates. *Hangin' Tough* would be the first cassette I would own. I had a NKOTB puzzle I put together, glued to poster board, and hung on my bedroom wall. I wore my NKOTB T-shirt as often as I could with tight-rolled, stonewashed jeans.

In my room, I displayed my prized possessions. I had a bear lamp which looked just like Mr. Bear. I had a HANG IN THERE cat poster. I loved unicorns—perhaps the girliest thing about me—and taped to my wall was a picture of the mythical beast that I had proudly drawn. My bed was covered with a unicorn comforter that was surprisingly gender neutral—all primary colors, no pink or pastels.

I loved to play records and dance in front of a full-length mirror. Madonna ruled.

My mom took me to get a haircut at a dingy shopping center salon, and too late I realized that I was getting the dreaded bowl haircut. I was devastated and cried, refusing to leave the house for several days.

When the Gulf War happened, I knew it was important and had a feeling that I needed to record what was happening. I sat in front of the TV for hours taking notes.

Around this time, I started documenting and saving many things. I had a vague notion that I was saving things to share with my future children, passing along a legacy of memories. I realize now that I was protecting my memories.

My mom would send me to buy cigarettes. The clerk looked at me like I was crazy but sent me home with them often enough for my mom to continue sending me to get them. With my own money, I would buy root beer wax candy, Werther's caramels, and Big-League Chew shredded gum.

I remember running down a dim hallway to answer the phone in the kitchen. I turned too soon and slammed into the wall. I only got a black eye this time.

18

For Halloween, I dressed up as a vampire. Mom put handfuls of Crisco in my hair to slick it back and I looked amazing. Happy and exhausted after trick-or-treating, I was ready to take a bath and go to bed. I climbed into the tub and tried to wash out my vampire hair, but the Crisco was so thick and greasy that the shampoo immediately lost all its bubbles.

I sheepishly called out to my mom to please come help me. When she came in, I could feel her annoyance like a wave descending into the bathroom. She reluctantly came over to the tub and poured more shampoo onto my hair, slowly massaging it in, then becoming rougher as the bubbles quickly faded away. The water turned greasy with chunks of Crisco floating at the surface.

Distressed, I looked at her face, still unfamiliar to me. I wanted to wrap my small arms around her neck and for her to tell me that it was going to be okay, but her look stopped me. I felt like a gross bug, so I pulled my arms close to my body and looked away as she drained and then refilled the tub.

The water was a few degrees hotter than the last and I bit my lip as I slipped back in. My scalp was sore from all the scrubbing and now my skin was greasy too. She poured more and more shampoo onto my hair and furiously massaged it in. We repeated this process a few more times, draining and refilling the tub with scalding hot water. My mom scrubbing me until my skin and scalp were raw. Finally, she gave up. Maybe she heard my whimpers or felt my constant tremble. Or maybe her arms were exhausted from all the effort.

With my hair still slightly greasy, I climbed into bed and tucked myself deep under my covers, my nose pressed against Mr. Bear as I held him tight. My jubilant Halloween adventure lost from thought, I slipped into a dreamless sleep.

19

Though I was part Asian, I did not look as ethnic as my sister. It set her apart and the local boys were cruel in their bullying. We had come from a home where our cousins were mixed from several races, so this unwanted attention was new and painful. I had to learn how-to beat-up boys to protect my little sister.

But I couldn't protect her from my mom. She had a rubber paddle (the kind you played ping pong with) that she never used on me but seemed to enjoy using on my sister. Once one of us brought lice home from summer camp and my sister was severely punished, her skin a web of crisscross patterns, like a human waffle. We both sobbed hysterically. Whenever possible, I would pick fights with my mom. If I stood a certain way and took a deep breath, I could make my voice big enough to distract her from my sister. But my fists weren't big enough back then.

Jill and I couldn't figure our mom out. Other moms gave hugs and said, "I love you," but the main emotion we seemed to get from her was anger. Otherwise, she was cold and cautious. I remember her telling me that if it weren't for us, she would never have to speak to my dad. But it didn't seem like she wanted to talk to us either.

My dad would call us once a week during *The Simpsons* (the hottest new show on TV) and we would be distracted. My mother purposely scheduled calls during that time and eventually they stopped. She told my dad that we didn't want to talk to him, while we believed he grew tired of us. Many years later, my sister would find a box full of unopened letters and packages my dad's family had sent during that time.

In contrast, my stepdad, Dan, was fun and playful with us. At least at the beginning. Dan was slim and only slightly taller than me. His dark curly hair was overgrown and unruly, and he had a large nose. It must have been quite an adjustment to suddenly become a dad. Did we take time away from him and my mom? Or did we bring him joy where there had been a void? I never did see my mom overly affectionate with him. She was often buried in her own tasks or hobbies.

He would become the only person to remember our birthdays and holidays. At that time, I think he was still in the honeymoon phase with my mom. My mom, who was beautiful and smart, could truly captivate an audience when she wanted to.

Mom cooked a lot that year. She would go through phases and prepare certain cuisines depending on her mood. She would make pasta from scratch, pan-seared calamari, and matzah balls. She would make Korean hot pot or Indian food. She cooked her way around the world in the apartment's small kitchen.

Aside from the culinary tour, my mom did do some kind things. When I'd lose a baby tooth, she pretended to be the Tooth Fairy and wrote me notes with a silver pen. I already knew Santa Claus was not real but there was something magical about this deception. Under the guise of night and myth, my mom attempted to connect with me.

I stayed up one night, tightly clutching the envelope containing my tooth. She tiptoed into the room as I pretended to sleep. I clutched the envelope so hard that we were soon in a silent tug-of-war. After a long time, she gave up. But the next morning, I found my note alongside a few coins. She must have stayed up for some time to win.

Sleep became a place of dread as the months passed. I remember two recurring nightmares in vivid detail. One had me trapped in a maze with the cast of *Sesame Street,* but they looked old and stained. At the end, a monkey with very long nails would stab me and I would wake up as I was dying. The other had me in a church where I was being held down by an invisible presence who seemed to get angrier and more aggressive with each passing second. I would scream but nobody could help me.

20

We moved out of the apartment building and into a single-family home in the next town over. The house had bars on the windows and sat on top of a hill in a cul-de-sac. It felt like a fortress. We had a large yard and the woods ran deep behind our neighborhood. This house was much larger than our cramped apartment. Maybe we could be happy here.

For the first time in my life, I had my own room.

That summer my sister and I went to day camp. I remember going to a water park where I tried to swim in the wave pool and kept getting knocked down and couldn't catch my breath. I remember the panic that set in. I learned to make friendship bracelets out of rubber strips. Those bracelets were like currency; we traded them for loyalty.

My stepdad was an engineer and would travel for work, leaving us alone with our mom. In between fights, she would mostly ignore us, and we tried to be invisible until he returned. He would bring back souvenirs from the places he visited. I especially loved a tin cup with a handle that he brought me from San Francisco. It had vertical black and white stripes and the word ALCATRAZ stamped on the side. He brought me currency from all over the world, which I still have to this day. When I was younger, I would close my eyes and pick a coin and promised myself that I would travel there one day.

We settled into our new home and my sister and I made friends in the neighborhood. During the day we were not allowed in the house and could only come home for meals and sleep. We played for hours in our suburban spaces and the surrounding woods. We built forts in those woods and stretched our imagination to their limits.

I clung to the other stay-at-home moms with small children, trying to make myself useful and sneak a bit of attention. I quickly became a trusted helper and started earning a couple dollars here and there. Soon enough, my babysitting career was launched and would help me meet loose ends for the next several years.

For play, we had Skip-It and an Atari video game console, with the former getting more wear and tear since our indoor playtime was limited. A kid in the neighborhood had a mini motorized car and I thought they were rich.

During heavy rainstorms the cul-de-sac would fill with water, and when the rain and lightning slacked off, we would grab our cheap donut floaties to glide on our backs in the shallow "pool." Toes dangling in the water, we used our arms as oars. We would laugh as we bumped into each other.

I found a batch of four-leaf clovers in the backyard and picked them all. I had a plastic Garfield wallet and put the clovers into the plastic slots meant for photos. Over the years I gave all but one away to people who seemed like they needed a little luck.

The woods behind our neighborhood caught fire and burned our forts down. The fire burned for hours and we watched the smoke slip into the horizon. A few weeks later, I walked through the debris and was surprised to find tiny green sprouts pushing through the ashes. I was deeply moved by the beauty and this is when I started to journal. I needed to put my intense feelings to paper.

We weren't allowed to watch *Full House*, as my mom said it was unrealistic that three men could raise those girls. She thought it was vulgar. But she let me watch *The Exorcist*, and when the girl's head twisted around, I ran into my bedroom screaming. I hid under my blankets and sang "Twinkle, Twinkle, Little Star" until I fell asleep. Mom never came to comfort me.

My IQ was tested at the beginning of middle school and I was placed into the gifted and talented program. In class, we all wrote a short story and mine was a surprisingly dark and mature piece of work for a ten-year-old. I called it *School's Out Forever...*

I was an honor roll student and invited into The National Junior Beta Club. I was excited for the big ceremony and thought that maybe this accomplishment would convince my mom to like me. I looked for her in the crowd but never saw her face. My spirit was too crushed to ask her why she did not come. We never spoke of it.

21

Only a year passed before we moved to yet another home, just a few blocks away. But it was far enough to a kid with no bike, with a new school year on the horizon.

I went to a YMCA summer camp. My friends and I would sneak past the property line when the camp counselors were not looking. One day we found a pile of tiny diary keys next to a rotted burlap sack deep in the woods. We were scared and excited, our breath quick and low as we told ourselves a story of previous girls sneaking back there. We imagined that they were kidnapped and killed and the man who did this took their diaries as trophies, leaving the diary keys behind as a warning to others who might trespass. We each took one, swearing to always remember the girls. I still have that key.

I had my first real crush on a counselor named Tucker. One day I dove into the pool and was mortified when I surfaced to find my strapless bikini top around my ankles.

At some point I started carrying around a book for people to sign and write notes. I was trying to keep track of the moments and people flying past me, school after school, city after city. Counselor Tucker signed that book and I died of happiness.

Our new house was a '70s-style rambler with wood paneled walls, orange shag carpet, and bright yellow walls in the kitchen. We had another large backyard with lots of green grass and tall trees.

The tone in this house was different. It was not required for us to be outside all the time. I do not remember being around my mom or stepdad often. My sister and I would spend hours watching *The Golden Girls*, *The Gary Shandler Show*, *The Tracey Ullman Show*, and *The Price is Right*.

We did do some things together. For family night out, we often went to B B's Po-Boys and Seafood. We loved this place and could not get enough fried shrimp. We had popcorn shrimp for appetizers and Po-Boys for entrees.

For my next birthday, I was allowed to pick the restaurant and my cake of choice. I chose Chinese food. My favorite part of the meal was the fortune cookies. I thought they would give me words of wisdom, guidance in this uncertain life. When we got home, my mother pulled out the makings for my favorite dessert: angel food cake with fresh strawberries and whipped cream.

I attended a new school and there was a boy who really liked me. He wasn't unpopular but he wasn't popular. We had gone to Pass Christian Middle School together and coincidentally moved to the same new school district. I know he had no control over it, but it still felt weird, like I was being followed. It somehow did feel comforting that I had moved somewhere new and a bit of my past was with me. I was not invisible, drifting from city to city with no anchor.

I do not have many pictures during these years. In my school picture from my 1991–1992 yearbook, I wore a white T-shirt with a vest—which I am sure came sewn together. In another, I wore my stepdad's University of Virginia sweatshirt which had shrunk in the dryer and became a favorite of mine.

I finally got a bike and rode it everywhere. The summer, before my thirteenth birthday, I had been riding back from a friend's

98

house and thought I was extra sweaty. But I had gotten my period, finally. I was obsessed with *Are You There God? It's Me, Margaret* and the ache to become a woman had been deep. I went to the grocery store with my mom and she bought me pads and strawberry ice cream. But we never talked about it. I used my own money to buy tampons.

I loved to read and would raid my mother's bookshelves. I read Michael Crichton, Stephen King, Anne Rice, J.R.R. Tolkien, and John Grisham. I often had a dictionary by my side to look up words I did not know. I read "Nancy Drew," "The Baby-Sitters Club," the Earthsea series, and any books with dragons. I wore my library card out. I even made my own library in my bedroom and a library card for my little sister and let her check books out. Penalties applied for late returns.

I had a Mormon friend. She was tiny, pale, and kind. Her family was nice, and I spent a good amount of time at her house. The family liked me and made an exception on a Sunday to let me hang out during family time. There was no TV or radio; the family just hung out together. It struck me as novel.

I spent the most time at my best friend Lucy's house, which was huge and impressive. We would have many scavenger hunts and the neighbors always humored us. At night we would grab flashlights and play manhunt. When the parents were not paying attention, we would play truth or dare (our go-to dare was streaking semi-naked), sneak out to skinny dip in the ocean, and put tampons in mailboxes of boys we had crushes on.

We went back to the DC metro area for the holidays. I loved the National Air and Space Museum where we would be allowed to buy astronaut ice cream. I enjoyed going to my step-grandparents' home because it was so warm and cozy and filled with tons of knickknacks, plants, and art. They also kept all the memorabilia from when their kids were little: comics, Lite Brite, a Ouija board, and plenty of dolls. It amazed me how an entire basement was filled with someone's childhood and mine could fit in a backpack.

We had a bunny named Clover who frequently ran away. She would dig holes under the fence and turn up in the neighbor's garage. I have scars on my arm from her trying to escape my arms. I remember feeling happy and sad every time she ran away. I was happy when she returned because I loved her but sad because I wanted to be out of that house too. If she could successfully escape, then maybe I could too.

Unbeknownst to my sister and I, our mom had stepdad were having issues. My mom had a miscarriage and it did not seem like they could recover from it as a couple. The lost baby broke them. My stepdad moved back to Virginia and my mother packed us up to start a new life in Alabama.

22

After the divorce, the now three of us moved to Mobile, Alabama, where my mom would go back to university for her undergraduate degree. We lived on campus, in a house with a sagging porch. The once white exterior was gray and chipped, the wood splintering in places from years of neglect. When you walked in there was a small living room and space for a dining room table, where a desk with a computer sat instead. I would play many hours of *King's Quest* and *Oregon Trail* on that computer.

We did not have a TV. Instead, we would listen to my boom box, making mix tapes, and calling radio stations to make requests. My sister and I danced a lot in that living room.

The kitchen was at the back of the house with an aluminum screen door that led to the backyard. We didn't bother to lock the door.

With her classes and string of boyfriends keeping her occupied, Mom was rarely home. Each night I would heat canned Dinty Moore stew on the old gas stovetop and warm up slices of bread in the oven. I would hand-wash the dishes and make sure the house was clean. I battled cockroaches and scrubbed and tried to keep our place nice.

I would mow our large, crooked yard- the aging lawn mower spitting rocks at my ankles, leaving bruises.

Our backyard pushed up against the woods and my sister and I would explore. We loved nature. Having grown up around woods our entire life, we felt confident and safe amongst the tall trees and small creeks.

One time we got very lost. These were not familiar woods and they stretched far. We wandered for hours, only breaking loose as the sun was about to set. We got home, shaken up. The house was empty, as usual, so we shook it off and made dinner and listened to music.

Under the kitchen sink were cleaning supplies and cheap liquor. I would have my newfound friends over and we would drink from the liquor and then fill the bottles back up with water. My mom never said anything and the strange men she brought home on occasion never said anything as they guzzled the diluted liquor down.

My mom dated a man that looked like Tim Curry. My sister and I were huge fans of the movie *Clue* and it misled us to like him. One night he was roughhousing with my sister and he broke her arm "on accident." There was also a guy who was tall and skinny with long, stringy hair that fell across his shoulders. He had a mustache.

During our ten months or so in Alabama, I grew up fast. I started smoking, drinking, had my first kiss, had my heart broken and broke a heart. My sister and I started spending time with our own friends as we clumsily grew up without parents around. I tried to raise us, making sure we had food, clean clothes, homework completed, and that we made it to school. I made sure that we made it safely through the parentless nights.

By then, I mostly wore baggy jeans, T-shirts and flannels. It was grunge, or as much as I could put together based on our limited budget. I wanted Dr. Martens, but we barely had enough money to keep the lights on and to buy groceries.

I still had my bike and rode it any chance I could. I had a new best friend and she had a filthy but friendly home. I felt safe there, with her family. It was fun and we laughed a lot. I remember going to the river with her family. We floated on inner tubes and soaked up sunshine in our bikini tops and cut-off jean shorts. She had lots of freckles.

One evening we sat in the backroom of her house, nestled on the couch between piles of dirty clothes and crinkled fast food bags.

"Do you have a light?" I mumbled as one of my mom's NOW 100s cigarettes dangled from my lips. My friend dug into her pocket and her movement rustled the piles around us to life. A cockroach squirmed its way out of a pant leg and onto my lap.

I breathed in, stopping my reaction of wanting to scream, and brushed it away like it was a piece of dust clinging to my pants instead of a terror inducing monster that I would have nightmares about later.

In the same motion, I turned the volume up on the boombox and "Gin and Juice" blared. Without skipping a beat, we started singing at the top of our lungs.

23

I was in my room listening to the radio and talking to a friend on the phone. Those days, I spent hours on the phone at night. I did not know that my mom was home and she came into my room as I was smoking a cigarette that I had stolen from her stash. She calmly looked at me and then asked me if I had her lighter. I said no and she left, closing the door behind her. I finished my cigarette and put it out in the Alcatraz tin cup that I now used as an ashtray.

One Friday night I hosted a huge party and we overflowed into every room, except my mom's. We drank the liquor without bothering to fill it back up and smoked cigarettes inside the house and on the front stoop. In the backyard, the boys played a passing out game called "Toby's World" and they passed out and panicked and laughed and kept playing.

We played "truth or dare" and I had my first kiss. My friends staged the scene and I knew it was coming. I liked this guy and we went to the eighth-grade dance together, a hot couple for a short amount of time. He broke up with me soon after and started seeing some other girl.

I ended up dating his friend. He was in high school and much too mushy for me. He wrote me a love letter with a huge heart and rose drawn in the middle, his words sprawling in the spaces around it. When I broke up with him over the phone my sister sang and danced the *Wayne's World* version of "Foxy Heartbreaker." We were laughing hysterically, and I had to hang up on him.

Reading the letter right now, I feel sad that I treated him so cruelly.

I had started developing a true physical reaction to intimacy. It made me feel sick and uncomfortable. How could anyone care about me with any seriousness (look at my parents)? There must be something wrong with them.

I tried to kill myself in that house. I sat alone in my room one night, a bottle of Tylenol in one hand and cheap liquor in the other. I set the liquor down on the floor as I cracked open the Tylenol bottle and dumped all the pills into my hand. I remember thinking only two things: Would my mom cry when she found me? Would she come to my funeral?

I swallowed the fistful of pills, chased it with liquor, and waited. I lit one of my mom's cigarettes and then another. I listened to Kurt Cobain sing "All Apologies," feeling anxious in the silent moments as I rewound the cassette to play the song repeatedly.

Nothing happened, so I eventually went to bed. I wasn't sure how to feel past the slight nausea I had from the cheap liquor and chain smoking. I suppose I did feel relieved because I didn't really want to die. But that moment in time would follow me like a small, dark cloud for many years to come. I felt guilty and ashamed that I tried to kill myself, that I could have left my sister alone.

I never spoke of it again until my senior year of high school. I was working at a diner and had started to see the world outside of high school. I began to meet people who shared secrets. Real secrets. My new friends weren't connected to the life where I had to pretend to be normal. Without judgment, I was able to make this confession.

But even then, when I told the story, I made a joke that I did not have a headache for days. I don't think I really acknowledged how disturbing this experience was until I saw the pain in my future therapist's eyes when I fed him that same line. My confession, once a cartoon bubble protruding from my lips, suddenly felt very real.

24

My stepdad's job landed him in Northern Virginia. It was 1994, my
freshman year of high school, and we moved there to live with him
after he and my mom reconciled following their first divorce. He
hadn't been able to get over my mom and she needed him to take
care of us, so we tried to be a family again.

We moved into a townhouse, where the walls of your
neighbor's home were pressed up against your own. We had lived in
apartments and shared walls before, but these houses seemed
strange, lined up like a life-size game of Monopoly.

What game were we now playing? That of a happy family?

I didn't think so, because my mom looked at me with
indifference when I told her, "If you don't let me move back to
Mobile, I am going to kill myself." As I said it, I realized that I
sounded like every teenager in every movie that didn't get their way.
But, unlike those teenagers, I didn't have the parent who was doing

something *for your own good* or *because we love you.* I just had the parent who looked at me like I was fly in her wine glass; like she was debating whether to dump her drink down the sink, or to fish me out and flick me to the ground.

Admittedly, a part of me was glad to be back in Virginia, close to family. Living down south was extremely isolating. The once a year trip for holidays did not suffice. I grew closer to my stepfamily and to my mom's family. It felt nice to cross the line from polite relatives to comfortable family hangouts. It felt good to know where the forks were and which plates we used for casual meals versus holidays. When we had sleepovers, it felt comfortable waking up first and turning on the TV or curling up with a book on the couch. Instead of lying in bed, waiting for the house to stir.

We had large family gatherings whether on my grandpa Lorenzo's Sicilian side, my grandma Grace's Korean side, or my stepfamily's Jewish side. Living down south for years had not exposed me to much diversity of thought, food, or culture, and it felt good to be back in a space where that was celebrated. I had missed my aunts, uncles, and cousins on my father's side where we represented a variety of backgrounds, including Asian, black,

Hispanic, and white. It had not hit me until then how tense it had felt in the south around race. I was exposed to southern culture which opened my eyes up to southern charm but also racial prejudice.

There was always an abundance of delicious food. It did not matter which holiday, there seemed to be twice as much for the number gathered. I loved watching the food preparation, eavesdropping on conversations, and eventually asking to participate. I loved people's reaction to the food and how the entire place would buzz around the homemade spreads. My passion for cooking and feeding people deepened at these family gatherings.

But under the surface, I still felt uneasy. It was hard to settle down and accept that we might be happy. My stepdad was a good person and I know he tried to be a good husband and stepdad. But my mom required all our attention. We watched her carefully, wanting to connect with her. She would sit in front of her computer for hours. The bookshelves and the floor surrounding her were overflowing with books, notebooks, and loose papers. She had her own fortress built in the corner of our living room. We could see her, but we could not reach her.

I started baking a lot during this time, pulling recipes from my mom's *Betty Crocker Cookbook*. I loved its worn pages, the challenge of baking, and the science behind it. I would spend hours in the kitchen, cleaning as I went, and reading books as the aromas filled the house.

Without meaning to, I found myself trying to play the role of mom again. I thought that if I baked, we would gather around and laugh and talk and love each other. But instead I found myself trying to be quiet as to not disturb anyone. Noise was still a big deal in my house. We tip-toed around, sat close the TV with the volume down, and shut doors softly.

Mom had her good and bad days. For a while, she did make dinner every night and we ate as a family. We had healthy meals with plenty of vegetables and glasses of milk. We would talk about our days, sometimes telling fun stories and sometimes sitting in silence.

When we were being silly, we would have farting contests and crack up laughing.

When it was bad, there would be screaming fights, meals left untouched, broken dishes, or one of us left at the table until we finished our meal.

My sister and I struggled with our mutual dislike of lima beans and chopped liver those days, and it seemed to infuriate my mom. I was more likely to push through and swallow every bite, but my sister struggled. On these nights, I knew at the beginning of dinner that I would be going to bed exhausted, mentally and emotionally destroyed by the fight I would end up having with my mom to deflect from my sister. She would yell at me about how worthless I was, how she did not want me, and how I was a failure.

Those moments, I wanted to go back to Mobile. Even though my mom was never around there, and we were dirt poor, I had still felt somewhat grounded there. I had friends who cared about me.

In this new town, the kids had all pretty much known each other since they were born. It was a small, tight-knit community and I was the new girl, the freak with a deep southern accent.

Then, to make matters worse, there was the incident.

25

A couple of months into my freshman year, a group of kids invited me into their circle. I had made a couple of other friends, who were also new to the school, but I was especially happy to have friends who knew the ropes. One day they suggested we take a walk in the woods, a mix of guys and girls. I shrugged and said, "Okay."

We walked for quite some time. When we stopped, one of the boys got super close. I could tell he wanted something from me. His hand hovered over his zipper. "C'mon just do it," he said. "Everyone does it." I remember not knowing where I was or how to get home. They were acting so casual. Was I just a prude from the south? Alarm bells sounded off in my head. My heart raced.

"He really, really likes you and this is what we do," one of the girls said. Taking my silence for consent, the boy put his hand on my shoulder. As he pressed firmly down, I awkwardly lowered to my knees as he unzipped his pants. The crunch of twigs and leaves was deafening.

He pulled out his already hard penis and pressed it against my lips, his hands finding the back of my head. I had no idea what I was doing as he began to thrust inside of my mouth. I had barely had my first kiss.

There was a musty smell that I wasn't sure came from him or the moss-covered trees around us. I focused on that smell, that smell became the seconds that stretched into minutes.

When it was over, I trailed out of the woods behind them, not knowing how to feel. Had I done the right thing? Was he my boyfriend now? Was I officially part of their group?

They told everyone what had happened in the woods. I could see them laughing, and the embarrassment became unbearable. Between my already stressful home life and being harassed at school, I had an anxiety attack. I was freaking out and one of my actual new friends came to my rescue. Neither of us had ever skipped a class before, but she got me out of there.

We ran out the school door and around the lake to her house. We were about to open her front door when we spotted her mom inside. Lucky for us, she was vacuuming and had her head down. We giggled nervously from the excitement of almost getting caught and decided to go to my place instead.

Both of my parents' cars were gone when we arrived so we assumed the coast was clear. We went inside and were chatting when I heard a noise coming from the master bedroom. I went upstairs and slowly opened the door. My stepdad had hurt his back at work and was resting in bed. My mom had picked him up and dropped him off, thus leaving his car at his office.

We stared at each other like deer caught in the headlights. Without saying a word, I closed the door, and my friend and I ran out of the house, then proceeded to freak out.

When I got home later that afternoon, nobody mentioned anything to me. I thought maybe my stepdad didn't tell my mom. That would have been a small mercy.

A couple of days later, I was called into my guidance counselor's office. "Your mom called to let us know that you skipped school," she said. I looked at her and told her about what was happening at home, but not about the incident in the woods. I couldn't bring myself to admit that. She was such a kind person, and she could tell I was shaken up. She let me off with a warning and a hug.

My mom never spoke to me about *why* I skipped school. She never talked to me about anything. I was beginning to feel that I was essentially invisible to her, except for those times that I was painfully not.

26

Without any adults I trusted at the time to talk to, I buried all my secrets deep. I didn't try to hurt myself again, though the urge was strong. Maybe I would have if I thought it might evoke some emotion from my mom, but I had learned that it wouldn't. It was a bizarre circle of emotions- me wanting to hurt myself because she showed me no emotion; me not hurting myself because I knew she wouldn't react. Her lack of emotion both tortured and saved me.

It seemed like I could not do anything to make my mom happy, and yet I craved her approval so much.

There was a rule that if I did not bring home a 3.5 + GPA then I would be grounded. I often brought home that or higher. I was in advanced math classes, ahead of most of my peers. I was in the National Honor Society and I repeatedly got the Physical Fitness award. When AP was introduced to my school, I was put into those classes alongside my GT classes. I lettered in academia. I loved school and learning and could easily grasp complicated concepts.

But the only time I received praise was in front of other people, when she wanted to brag about me.

I was grounded a lot. Many times, my mom would forget my punishment as she went back to ignoring me. I learned to read these situations and would escape as much as possible. I was making friends and had people I could depend on outside of our home. But my mom hated that too, and if I mentioned hanging out with friends, she would ground me.

So, I would talk about studying and I joined after school activities, so I had a reason to not be home. If I had to be home, I used the computer as an excuse to have friends over. I would say that we had an important school assignment due and I was the only one with a computer. I tied everything back to grades, back to the only thing she seemed to care about.

I got to know my neighborhood and asked around about babysitting gigs. I found a steady one quickly and would spend the next couple of years babysitting frequently after school. I watched a sweet little girl who loved to play and to watch *Barney*. I would do my homework and dread the moments when I would have to walk back to my own home. Sometimes I would hang out after her mother returned home. We would sit around and chat. She had a real interest in who I was, and I welcomed the unfamiliar kindness she bestowed upon me.

One night I came home, and my mom was angry with me. I can't remember why. I only remember her hands wrapped around my neck. My socks slipping against the white and black kitchen tiles, causing me to drop to my knees and then slide onto my back. She stood over me, her face right in front of mine, feet planted firmly on either side of me. She pressed hard against my throat, throwing all her weight forward, as if she was about to do a handstand. With me as her base.

27

I was thin back then, 5'4" and weighed 95 lbs. Food had become such a challenging thing in my life, as we had moments of feast or famine. At times we struggled financially. Other times, my mom and stepdad forgot to feed us as their fights raged late into the night. Even when it quieted down, we would stay in our rooms, not wanting to put ourselves in danger of an unprovoked fight.

We were also punished by being deprived of food or by being forced to eat food we deeply despised. If we didn't, the fights would erupt.

Our grocery list rarely changed these days. We were back to a steady diet of frozen vegetables—lima beans and the mixed vegetables with the crinkle cuts. Dinty Moore was still a staple, along with Vienna sausages, tin canned oysters, crackers, oatmeal, store brand cereals, mac and cheese, and hot dogs. We had bologna and always wheat bread, never white.

It was around this time that my eating disorder started to take form. I didn't think I was overweight. It wasn't about weight. It was about the satisfaction I felt as I began to physically disappear, as I began to outwardly match how I felt on the inside. Eventually I lost my appetite for food and only took interest in how little I could eat. I would count the bites, calories, and fat. I would obsess over how little I could eat and still survive.

"Is that all you are having for dinner?" my sister would ask as I heated up a slice of bologna in the microwave. I could hear tiny bubbles of fat burst as the cold cut became burnt and chewy. I soaked up the grease with a paper towel before cutting the bologna into tiny slices.

I pretended to scan the pantry for more food, my fingers running lightly over cans of Dinty Moore and smoked oysters, over my mom's box of wine. My fingers twitched as if the Crisp White Franzia wine was about to spill out of the glass pictured on the side. I brought my fingers to my lips as I said, "Yeah, there isn't anything good in here anyway."

I went to the doctor for a sprained ankle and they found something unusual in my left heel bone. I had an advance cyst in the bone, running through all the chambers. It was so unusual that the doctor called other doctors in to look at the x-rays. They had not seen this before.

I was scheduled for a follow-up appointment after my ankle healed. I had been advised to be very careful to not put too much pressure on my feet. I tiptoed around like a ballerina.

My mom and I pulled into the parking lot and as I went to shut the car door, I did not move my hand out of the way fast enough. I screamed and yelled "MOM! MOM! MOM!" but she did not turn around. She was casually walking toward the front door. I screamed louder. The pain was intense, and I couldn't slide my caught finger out. Several seconds passed and other people in the parking lot were looking at me with concern.

She finally turned around as she realized that I was not walking next to her. I was still screaming and crying at this point and told her my finger was locked in the door and to please unlock it. She walked over, more curious than anything, and I was finally loose.

We spent the first part of my appointment burning a hole through my pinky nail to drain the fluid and relieve pressure. My nail would eventually become loose like a tooth and I wore Band-Aids on it until it finally fell off and until the nail grew back.

I ended up going through three painful procedures my freshman year to try to fix my heel bone. None of them worked and despite earlier warnings of caution against sports, I was advised that I should be fine after all.

As abruptly as I had become the center of attention, it ended. I went on to play sports, but I have always favored my right foot, slightly terrified that one misstep could shatter my other heel.

That summer my mom sent my sister and I to stay with my grandpa and new step-grandma in the mountains of North Carolina where they had retired.

My grandpa was now *the former* abusive alcoholic who had tortured my grandma Grace, aunt, and mom growing up. His new wife was a timid lady. The house was nearly silent. Jill and I's muscle memory activated the moment we walked through the front door. Must blend into the scenery, avoid detection.

One day he took my sister and I fishing to one of those small lakes that are purposefully filled with fish so people like my grandpa Lorenzo could fish and feel accomplished by their catch at the end of the day. We brought our fish home and his wife baked them in tinfoil sans any seasoning. They were bland and the bones brittle, but we ate them.

During most days, my grandpa Lorenzo would leave us at the pool for hours. I got so tan that summer that my friends hardly recognized me upon my return.

He had developed a deep distrust for the government. One night he asked me to take a walk with him after dinner, and my mind raced as I tied my shoes. We never spent actual time alone together and I did not want his undivided attention. *Where was this going?*

We stepped outside and my grandpa Lorenzo started talking about television and how it's corrupt. He started talking about different shows, messaging, and how it's all a conspiracy to make young people have sex. I had been half listening to his rant, but this stopped me. I think he was trying to have *The Talk* with me, but it was coming from a weird, uncomfortable place that I did not understand. I nodded and agreed and promised to not be influenced by these messages.

The weeks stretched on and it felt like we would never be returned home. I felt that familiar panic and loss of control. We did eventually go home but I refused to ever go back to visit them.

28

After being humiliated by the episode in the woods, I was shy at the beginning of my sophomore year. I managed to make a couple of friends, but I tentatively walked the halls and quietly took up space in class. I was bubbling under the surface though. I had so much to say, so much laughter to share, so much hurt that I needed to release, so much creativity to explore. The day simply came when I knew that I could not be contained anymore. I walked up to a group of girls, confidently introduced myself, and asked to sit with them at lunch. I repeated this in my classes, and I smiled at people and I spoke out loud and I felt alive.

I am not sure if I was putting on a mask and became this shining person or my shining person was able to come out because I put on the mask. Was I brave on the outside or the inside first? Either way, I quickly made lots of friends and threw myself into my classes and extracurricular activities.

My mom enrolled in a new university. Her focus was on engineering and she was excited to start the year. I liked the times when she seemed happy and interested in life. Those were the days she'd shower and leave the house. She might even make dinner and listen to how our days went.

She started slipping away quickly though, spending long hours at school. When she was home, she was planted in front of the computer in the makeshift office that had once been our dining room. Piles of papers and books were now stacked higher on the shelves and ground, impenetrable by us. She worked obsessively and the tiny clicks of the keyboard could be heard at all hours. At night, if I came downstairs for a glass of water, I would see her face floating in the darkness, lit green from the endless commands feeding onto the screen.

It seemed we all wanted to make this work, but my mom was the wild card. We tried to carefully watch her moods, anticipate scenarios that would set her off so we could steer clear of any drama. But, even more difficult, was managing the times when her mood seemed neutral, and she seemed uninterested in our lives. This made me feel like an inanimate object, just taking up space around her.

Space that she would rather use to stack more books, to build a higher wall to keep the outside world out.

Some days I curled up on the couch and read her books. I thought that if I could get her to see that we had common interests, she might want to talk to me. My reasoning: If she didn't love me as her daughter, maybe she could at least like me as a *peer*. That we could meet on an intellectual ground if not an emotional one.

I would sit on the couch because there, I was somewhat in her peripheral vision. It wasn't quite in her space, but I knew she could see me out of the corner of her eye. Maybe she would hear me as I crinkled the pages to turn them. But she rarely turned her head and I would eventually slide off the couch and quietly walk up the stairs to my room.

Eventually I stopped tiptoeing around. The explosive fights that had reverberated through the house erased that rule from the books. When they first got back together and we moved back in with my stepdad, for a short time things were pleasant. But within months they were back to fighting so loud the neighbors could hear from the sidewalk, through the walls. When the police knew you by name because of your parents' fighting, it was okay to slam the oven door.

So, when I cooked meals, I tried to be as loud as possible, as if the noise of my domestication would rouse her motherly instincts. It never did. I thought, *what if I broke this plate against the floor and picked up a shard? What if I cut myself with it and bled all over the kitchen? Would she get up and walk the few steps from her desk to check on me? What would it take to get her attention?*

My stepdad was growing increasingly frustrated and the days of him defending my mom were ending. The living room was now her bedroom and the adjoining dining room (turned office) was her whole world, besides the hours she spent at school. I imagine he felt the pressure to raise us without her. She didn't grocery shop, remember birthdays, or do anything for the family. She was cruel or distant mostly.

But sometimes she would seem so sad that all I wanted to do was to hug her and tell her I loved her no matter what. I knew that if she said *I love you* just one time to me, I'd forgive her for everything. But she never did. The space in my heart that has never held an *I love you* from her is empty and dull. One time I tried to play a congo and my hand fell flat against the drum; the sound didn't echo or vibrate, and my hand stung a bit. I thought, *this is what that empty space feels like.*

I know that my stepdad felt pain. He often confided in me about their problems. Even though I was only fifteen years old. Even though he ignored mine.

For years, he had been in love with my mom. I imagine that it was exhilarating to be in love with her. She was beautiful, artistic, and book smart. She was standoffish and girlish, somehow controlling the room and a damsel in distress in the same moment. My mom wanted to possess you but never touched you. Most of all, she knew you- your faults and your best qualities. She knew with perfect timing when and what to say to build you up or break you down, grandpa Lorenzo had taught her well. She would remain unchanged as you withered and crumpled in front of her. When I told her, "I love you," she returned no sign of recognition or affection.

29

I tried to live a normal teenage life as I immersed myself in school and activities. I even made the JV cheerleading squad. While I was excited to be a part of a team and to make new friends, I felt significantly out of place. I didn't have product or a curling iron. My mom didn't give me these things or consider I needed them, and I never asked her. Instead, I borrowed her blow dryer that she barely used. I didn't have a proper brush, so I'd end up with a pile of thick, frizzy hair I'd cram into a ponytail. My stepdad took care of all the shopping, even buying the house supply of feminine products. We never asked for these things, he just got them for us. I felt like asking for anything more would be asking for too much. I didn't want to push.

Having perfect hair wouldn't have mattered, though. There was still something deep inside me that resisted *dolling up*. The little girl who played in the mud and muck in her Cinderella gown. When

I applied lip gloss, my first urge was to wipe it right off. I felt like I was playing dress up and couldn't imagine that I looked attractive at all. I wondered if any of the other girls felt this way, or if I was just a freak. I watched the other girls get ready, trying to follow suit as I daydreamed about jeans and T-shirts while I adjusted my cheerleading skirt to be as short as theirs.

Suddenly, because of cheerleading, I started becoming *visible* and I was getting lots of attention. The cheerleaders wore their uniforms every game day. It was the beginning of being stared at, assessed, approached by strangers, and processing comments from boys and girls. I tried to act sophisticated and sexy, but I had always been awkward and clumsy. After all those years of craving visibility and attention from my mom, I had it in the outside world and would soon realize that I didn't know what to do with it

On game day, the football players gathered around their lockers. The other girls were always at the top of their game, so I generally tried to be sexy. Any one of these guys could have been a teen heartthrob on a poster hanging on my wall, but then again, they all kind of looked the same. I still couldn't remember who was who if they weren't wearing their distinctive ball caps (they served as name tags to me). I mentally dubbed these guys as the *generic boys*.

Some had been part of the crowd that had mercilessly teased me after the incident in the woods the year before. Since then, I had come out of my shell, started making friends, and now I was a cheerleader. Now they were paying attention to me in a new way, curious as to who I was.

One day, when it was time to head out for the game, I was laughing and waving to friends as I walked away. As I faced forward, I ran directly into a huge pole. The *thud!* of my head meeting the cement was audible to the surrounding crowd. I fell to the ground, more out of embarrassment than pain. I wanted to shrink away as our bowtie-clad counselor raced toward me to see if I was okay.

"I'm okay!" I said as I threw my hands up in protest of needing to see the school nurse. I pretended to flip hair over my shoulder and confirmed, "I'm, like, totally okay!"

Everyone laughed and we made jokes the rest of the night. It became a legendary story. The guys thought it was cute, and I embraced the wide-eyed, giggly demeanor to which they seemed to respond best. I soaked in the attention. It felt like I had cracked a code (along with my head). It was okay to be clumsy and awkward if you were ditzy and cute.

Inside, I questioned what I was doing, but quickly shushed that voice. I was playing a part to fit in. I was wearing a new face. It wasn't a brave face, but it was still a mask I could hide behind. What was the difference if it was helping me survive? If it was making me less invisible? I started to collect those moments of attention and save them up for later, when I was at home and being ignored. It was comforting to know somewhere in the world I could be seen.

Unfortunately, I didn't care about who was giving me attention. I would only later learn that this would create a different feeling of invisibility for me. I would learn that having someone love, or even just like you, for one of the masks you were wearing could be unbearable. That the weight of that mask would suffocate you. But the terror of taking it off was even worse. Because underneath was a mess of scars and tears. Who could possibly want that? But at this time in my life, the attention was a tourniquet I tied tight to help keep myself alive.

During this time, I developed a pattern that would follow me well into adulthood. Once I received attention, I immediately wanted it to go away if the attention started to feel intimate. I would see this unfold in every relationship I entered, even as I dated the most popular boys in school. I just needed the outside world to see that I was getting attention from them. I would freeze up if they asked me on dates, trying to think of who we could double date with, or I would use homework as an excuse to not go out. It wasn't that I didn't like them. I enjoyed them *as friends*. But emotionally intimate moments made me panic.

One of my friends had an older brother who was a senior. We were the annoying but fun younger girls and we would tag along with him and his friends as often as we could. I liked being around the older guys. They looked out for us and it felt safe being with them.

I ended up dating one of his friends after I quit cheerleading and joined the swim team with them. I had only joined cheerleading to support my friend and she was now happily settled into the team. I felt like I would rather die than continue to basketball season, as being on display had made me feel deeply self-conscious. I was excited to now be part of a team that wore tracksuits on game day. This was the perfect opportunity for me to ditch the short skirts, be around friends, *and* have an excuse to not be home.

The swimmer I dated was sweet and caring and stood by me as my home life fell apart that sophomore year. I still have the letters and emails he wrote to me, and I read them sometimes to try to understand who I was during that time in my life. I feel like he really understood and valued me, through our friendship, dating, and breakup. He wasn't the only person in my life that I feel this way about, but he was the one that I would most frequently talk to about it, out loud or on paper.

In one letter, he wrote: *But seriously, you're a great person and we share some history too. All those long morality talks about honesty and judgments were a lot of fun. Me and you are on the same level and we share a lot of personality traits too. I like you because we can talk forever and not get bored. You're real levelheaded, you see things for how they are, and you don't dodge serious conversation. You're mature but you can still mess around and have fun. You're a great person to make fun of but you can dish it out with the best of them. (I hope you're smiling now.) You're*

138

smart and sincere. You are healthy and take care of yourself. I know this isn't supposed to be important, but I'll put it in anyways… You actually have a great body and a pretty smile. I've always had a great time flirting with you and you are SEXY, DAMN!

He really cared for me, which was evident in his letters, but I ended up hurting him. I kept him close for almost a year, but I also pushed him away.

In another letter he wrote: *You're a really special person to me, I guess that's why I don't care about the mistakes you make. I know the real you and that's what I see, it's all I see.*

And I believe that he did see me. But logically I couldn't believe it was possible, not from a friend or a boyfriend.

30

I continued to make more friends through sports and school, and it felt amazing to be seen and heard. I was gaining confidence by discovering who I was as a person. It enthralled me to develop my own ideas about life and discuss them with others during breaks or in class. I was becoming *popular* but had friends from different cliques.

As my sophomore year progressed, a new hot topic arrived: obtaining a driver's permit. I could hide most things from my peers, but not having my permit was a difficult thing to explain away. At first, I could explain that my parents were busy but eventually I would have to admit, "My parents won't teach me to drive." Any follow-up questions would have to be answered with, "They won't teach me because my mom hates me, and my stepdad doesn't want me to ruin his car." He'd made it clear I was not learning in his prized Toyota Celica.

Every time I asked my mom, "Will you please teach me to drive?" it pained me, knowing she would likely say no. I had been able to hack my own way through other obstacles, but I needed an adult for this milestone. I needed my parents.

Resigned to the fact that I would have to bum rides for the rest of high school, I told myself I could hold out until the freedom of turning eighteen in a couple of years. My mental calendar had been counting down the days for a while, looking forward to the day I could take control of my own life. I imagined the day I could leave home, then petition for custody of my sister. Being eighteen meant that life would be easy and could be fair.

Then, after an especially hard snowfall that had kept us home from school, my mom cheerfully called up for me to grab my coat. She was going to teach me to drive! Glancing out the frosty window, I felt the hairs on the back of my neck rise. The roads were barely cleared, and children were sliding every which way as they threw snowballs at each other.

My mom had a small, stick shift Toyota Tercel. I was no expert on cars but was certain this was basically the worst car to drive in the snow. But as she had barely spoken to me in weeks, and this opportunity to be alone with her while she was in a good mood might not come again any time soon, I decided the risk was worth it.

The day was bright and sunny, and she drove that tiny car out of our neighborhood like it was a monster truck. Watching her pull that off, I thought maybe I was wrong. Maybe this was, in fact, the best car for driving in this type of weather.

She took a left turn into the empty parking lot of a government building which had been lightly plowed. We switched places and I barely had to adjust the seat and mirrors. It made my skin tingle to realize we were having a mom and daughter moment, and I felt something like affection. It made me feel special and connected to her. Her teaching me to drive was a milestone, like a dad teaching his son to shave. This gave me a sense of feeling grown up. Of being like her.

That the mirrors were at my level also gave me a sense that we were *matched* in a way. That she wasn't *above* me, the way you think when you're a kid and you must look up to see your parents. Something about that moment made me feel that I wasn't less than her, though deep down I knew I wasn't going to be able to impress her. Not even a little. Still, she had never taught me anything before, and somehow, even just for this fleeting moment, she rated me as worthwhile to teach.

She lit a cigarette and began the lesson. "Let the clutch up as you push down on the gas pedal. You'll feel it catch."

Um, okay, I thought to myself, not really knowing which the brake, clutch, or gas was. I didn't want to ask her because any sign of ignorance usually set her off. I nodded like I knew exactly what she meant and starting pumping pedals. The snow and ice gave me a bit of an excuse as we jerked forward.

Surprisingly, I picked it up quickly. But the car was no longer a monster truck and we were soon sliding out of control. The tires spun out and the rear of the car swished back and forth, as if dancing to music. My empty stomach heaved against the motion and when I went for a deep breath, I got a mouthful of secondhand smoke.

We finally came to a stop. Trying to not throw up, I said in a light tone, "Thanks for the lesson. Ready to switch back and go home?" Not noticing my distress, she insisted that I keep going. Despite my nerves being shot, I did as I was told.

The windows were fogging up from our breath and body heat and the smoke had no place to escape besides into our lungs. My hands were clammy under my thick gloves as I gripped the wheel. "Okay, now you are going to switch to second gear," she said, "so you'll need to gain a bit more speed."

Lightheaded and panicked, I crept forward again. I gained speed and when I went to shift into second, the car spun completely out of control, doing donuts at what felt like breakneck speed. I heard a *crack* and the car slowed down, the nose finally pushing up against a snow pile after knocking down a parking lot sign.

Jumping out of the car, I was certain there were cameras watching us and police would be at the scene any moment. I steadied myself for Mom to yell at me as I searched her car for damage, but miraculously there was none. My mom was nonchalant as she kicked the sign out of the way, got into the driver's side, and drove us home, the car a confident monster truck once more.

31

Drama really began to escalate in our home a few weeks later. Many nights I would come home only to turn back around to run to a friend's house, who lived a couple blocks away. A knock at their door was the only heads-up her family needed. They knew from my swollen, red eyes that I cried along the short path that led from my doorstep to theirs, and that I needed a safe place to sleep and a few hugs to calm my racing heart.

Mom had started to become upset about phone calls she received at home. I had answered once and an older man asked for her, identifying himself as her professor. Taking the call and speaking with him, she sounded upset and hung up on him. It seemed odd to me but then again, it took a lot to raise a red flag when it came to my mom.

A short time later, she told us that she was kicked out of university because her professor had been stalking her. When she went to report him, they reversed the accusation and said it was her who had been stalking him and they expelled her.

She was furious at the situation and refused to let it go. My mom filed a lawsuit against the university, and for months it became her obsession to win. She wanted to destroy those men and bring the university to its knees. But it was the final nail in the coffin for our family. We were not going to survive this intact.

Our cat, whom I named Baby, was the first to go. He was a black and white stray, and he came and left the house as he pleased. Our relationship was simple. I fed and pet him and he, in turn, cuddled up next to me. He'd spend hours lying on my chest, his paws wrapped around my neck in a tiny hug, kneading my hair as he purred. The vibrations from his purring pushed against my ribcage and sank into my heart. I thought about the ease of loving this little animal, how much joy it brought me to care for him. It made me wonder why my mom took no joy in caring for our family, or why she never wanted to touch or be touched. If only she could show me just a fraction of the love this cat offered me. I would take that and not feel like such a failure, so unlovable.

After Baby hadn't come home for several days, I searched the neighborhood. That's how I learned he'd adopted another family. A nice family. Jealousy consumed me when I watched this family petting him as I peered through the window. I didn't blame Baby. Unlike Patches, he wouldn't be abandoned to die alone. He left first, perhaps sensing my emptiness and the dysfunction that surrounded us. He'd found a new place to be safe and happy, and I hoped he'd left because he'd felt the unease, and not betrayed by me.

Back home, my mom was on edge as she poured over law books, case studies, and consulted anyone who would speak with her. She preferred to build her own case versus hiring a lawyer, trusting her ability over theirs. To her credit, my mom was focused, smart, and methodical as she built her case. But it became maniacal and repetitive after a few weeks.

I stopped sitting on the couch. I no longer wanted to be in her periphery. "What did my professor say to you when he called?" She would look at me expectantly, but I had nothing to give her. At first, I would have given my left arm to give her a piece of information, anything to get her to look at me, talk to me. But I had nothing to share. "He just asked for you," was all I had to offer.

My mom started to become even more paranoid. She had been diagnosed with manic depression, and I suspected that she was off her meds. Her clothes stiffened around her, her unwashed hair thick with grease, as she pushed forward in her lawsuit. My answers seemed only to irritate her. Instead of seeing me as a potential ally, she looked at me like I was working with the enemy. She would often say, "This world is against me. You are all against me."

A part of me *was* mortified that my mom was suing a college that my friends' siblings attended, and one that was on my list to apply to come senior year. But a part of me also believed her. She was beautiful and I saw how men reacted to her. I wasn't sure which story I believed, and I felt guilty for that. But I didn't know who she was outside of the walls of our home, or inside for that matter, and I didn't know these men she was battling against.

I couldn't connect to her. I couldn't understand her. So how could I side with her? Except that she was my mom and I wanted all these things; I just didn't know where to even begin. So, I remained neutral.

What I was sure of was that my stepdad was ready to leave, and I had no idea what we would do if left alone with her again. The eight months with her in Mobile had exposed her inability to care for us on her own, leaving us to fend for ourselves as she disappeared for days. My stepdad was not much of a shield against her attacks but at least he made sure our basic needs were met.

Weeks passed and one day my frustration boiled over as she pressed me again about the call with the professor. I realized once and for all that she did not care about us, how we were doing, or if we were safe or happy.

"Stop!" I screamed at her. "We don't deserve this! You need to take your meds and start being a part of this family. Why did you even take us from my dad in the first place?" I couldn't contain the rage and hurt that had been bottled up inside of me. For once, I wanted her to hear me, see me, answer me. There had to be something inside of her that could feel empathy, something that recognized that she was my mom and I her child. Was there not the smallest thread of connection from her being to mine?

"You are such a little bitch," she replied.

"No, *you're* the bitch." My words were like a hammer against the eggshell floor I had been walking on for years. I knew I was about to break something that could never be fixed.

I watched her carefully, trying to gauge her reaction, like I always did. Usually her expression didn't change, but this time her eyes shifted, and it scared me. I could tell she was coming for me. I turned and ran up the stairs to my bedroom. I tried to shut and lock the door, but she was right behind me. She flung the door open and pushed me. My back hit my bed hard, knocking the wind out of me.

I had my bear lamp on my bedside table, the one I got when I was nine. The bear sat on a wood base with a rod that went through to the top of its head to meet the light bulb. The lamp shade looked like a hat and was decorated with bears and balloons. He looked like a cousin of Mr. Bear, whom I still slept with at night. My sister had a matching one, and even though I had probably outgrown the lamp, I still loved it.

My mom picked up the lamp and raised it above her head. Her eyes were wild, and her jaw clenched. Her small frame was coiled tight.

I twisted around just in time for the lamp to hit my back. She hit me so hard that the rod separated from the wood base, the shade ripped, and the bulb shattered. I saw her lift it above her head again, and I knew she would keep raising that lamp and crashing it against me. I then remembered sitting in the driver's seat of her car, and that I almost matched her size. I realized; I was not a little child anymore. I wasn't going to allow her to strike me again.

As I saw the jagged edges of the lamp coming toward me, I kicked hard and made contact with her stomach. She went flying back as she dropped the lamp and I was able to scramble to my feet, willing myself to stand as tall as I could. My fists were clenched, and my feet were planted. I looked at her in a way as to leave no doubt that I would fight for myself, for the life that she seemed determined to shred apart.

She looked at me warily as she began to understand me.

"Don't *ever* lay a hand on me again," I warned, my voice shaky but bold. "Don't ever touch my sister again. Get out of my room. RIGHT. NOW."

We stared at each other, both breathing heavily. She slowly backed up and closed the door behind her. Avoiding the glass on the floor, I crossed the room to lock the door. I picked up the mangled lamp and cried as I cradled it in my lap.

32

Several weeks later, my mom disappeared. We hadn't much contact since *the incident*, acting stiffly polite around each other if we happened to pass in the hallway. I was staying away as much as possible, burying myself into schoolwork, friends, and other people's families.

My sister and I came home from school one day and her car was there, but she was nowhere to be found. I looked for a note but found none, not that she'd ever leave one. But she had not been leaving the house much, if at all lately. She was in a losing battle with the lawsuit and I wondered if she finally cracked and tried to make good on the suicide threats she had occasionally made to my stepdad, who then mentioned them to me. I went upstairs, risking getting caught in my parents' bedroom, to see if anything was missing, but all her clothes and personal belongings were there. My heartbeat unevenly as I backed out of the room.

My sister and I could do nothing but sit on the couch and wait for my stepdad to come home. When he did, he quietly opened the front door as if he were a teenager, sneaking back in after a night out. We sat there, roles reversed, as if we were worried parents wringing our hands, and had been up all-night calling hospitals and police stations. My heart was pounding when I asked him, "Where's our mom?"

He looked away and mumbled, "I don't know." But I knew he was lying. He seemed embarrassed and mad. It reminded me of years before when an ambulance had taken my mom to the hospital and we sat in the ER awaiting news. He told us she had just gotten sick. We sat there for hours as she recovered from what we thought was a cold, but was really a miscarriage, as I found out years later. When they released her, my sister and I made her get-well cards and tried to take care of her. She let us near her at the time, just for a little bit.

But now she was wasn't in the hospital with a "cold." Now she'd left us.

In the days that followed, my stepdad avoided eye contact with us. He seemed to forget that we were children that needed and loved him. Finally, he told us, "You aren't my legal children. I have no responsibility for you."

This was the man who had shown up in Ohio in 1989, with my mom, leaving his shiny red car at the bottom of the driveway. He still had that car, more pink than cherry red now from years in the hot summer sun. He had been our stepdad for the past six years, the one who remembered our birthdays, made plans for the holidays, and took care of us. But he had never adopted us.

He had been the one witness to what happened behind closed doors with our mom. By abandoning us, he was destroying evidence and dismantling our credibility. He had been an accomplice to my mom taking us away from my dad and to what happened to us over those years by silently standing by, but he never did have the courage to own up to that.

My sister and I were on our own to survive.

Even though we had a big family, everyone seemed to suddenly disappear. It was as if my mom had taken them with her, to a faraway place we couldn't find. I spent hours dialing numbers on my pink touch tone-phone, but few answered, and if they did, it seemed like they couldn't hear me. Calls ended with, "Okay, well let us know if you need anything" and "Keep us posted."

Didn't they realize I *was* letting them know what I needed and soon I might not have a phone to call them on and keep them posted? Our stepdad was making us leave the house. He was going to stay there for a while, then sell it so we needed to clear out. I was fifteen at the time and my sister was thirteen.

My sister and I both told our stories to our best friends. My sister had a friend in the neighborhood whose mom loved her and said she could stay as long as she needed. I had grown close to my best friend's family and they knew quite a bit about my home life. Her mom would hug me and call me names like *honey* and *sweetheart* and told me she loved me. I had never known that moms could be that way.

When my friend told her parents what was happening, she asked if I could move in with them, and they said "Of course." They had two children in high school, and that must have been a tremendous decision for them to make, yet they did so quickly, insistently. They wanted to protect and love me.

My heart ached as my sister and I packed our favorite possessions and clothes. Again. The past was suddenly right in front of us as we looked at the stuff we would leave behind. And this time it wasn't just our things we would have to say goodbye to. We also had to say goodbye to each other.

We were going our separate ways and I was scared for her. I knew that I was going to a safe place and felt guilty about that. I didn't know her friend's family, and if they could protect her like I had. I thought again about my plan to get custody of her once I turned eighteen, yet that moment seemed like an eternity away. She looked to me to protect her, but I couldn't this time. I had been reaching into my toolbox to try to fix this situation, but it was empty, my fingers scraping against cold metal.

All I could do was hold her hand as long as I could. "Jill, it's going to be okay. This is just going to be temporary." But I could feel the lightness of those words, ready to float away from us. I remembered my dad saying the same thing to us all those years ago. My sister didn't look like she believed me.

"We've survived worse, right?" I said.

But had we? Not answering that question, we looked into each other's brave face before we took our final steps out of the house. The emptiness inside was like a vacuum, slamming the door shut behind us.

33

Just as I was settling into my new home, I received a call from Mom. I had left the number of where I would be in the kitchen, with a note saying I would be staying with them. It was a bit ridiculous, leaving a note for a person who had disappeared and for another who was there but didn't care about me, but I had left it all the same.

It turns out that my mom had checked herself into a mental institution. She experienced a breakdown from losing the lawsuit and had been suicidal. She was calling to tell me that she had checked herself out and was coming to pick me up. She made no mention of my sister; it was just me she was coming for.

The walls of the room seemed to tumble toward me, the air sucked out of the room. "I'm coming to pick you up," she said again. I used my remaining oxygen to plead, "I'm happy here. Can't I just stay here? They love me and don't mind at all." I tried to convince her that it was better for her too. "Take the time to recover and feel better. Try to make things better with your marriage."

"I'll be there soon to get you," she said. I hung up the phone and cried in my friend's mom's arms. I had finally felt safe somewhere and the thought of going back to my mom gave me the sensation of being buried alive.

I hoped she wouldn't show that she was just going to disappear again after her call, but of course I knew better. Her need to possess me, to control me, was strong. I was hers, even if all she did was try to break me. She treated me like a toy. I belonged to her, and nobody else could touch me unless she said so.

I had engaged Child Protection Services when I moved in with my friend's family. The cops who frequented our house in response to my parents' fighting never seemed too concerned with us, so this was the first that I had heard of an agency that was supposed to look out for children's well-being.

I was skeptical at first since my sister and I had been neglected by court systems and the police so many times. But we needed a record of what was happening and to make a case for me to stay with them when my mom resurfaced. I told them about her disappearance, that I didn't know where she was, and that I suspected she was off her meds and suicidal. They advised me to call the police if she showed up. Which we did.

I felt the panic rising when I spotted her through the front window. "She's here," I said. She looked out of place against the nicely manicured lawns and spring flowers that had just bloomed. She looked very thin, the type of thin I was constantly striving for. She looked like she had something terrible in her, eating her from the inside out.

My friend's parents opened the front door for my mom as I hid in the kitchen. They were polite but firm. "I'm sorry, but you cannot come in and Persephone is not going with you. We have called the police because we are worried about her safety."

I could hear my mom say, "She is MY daughter" over and over, her voice eventually muffled by the closing of the door.

When the police showed up, I gave them my account of what had happened over the past several months. I could see the regret in the policeman's eyes as he told me, "I'm sorry but it's out of our hands. She is your mother and you have to go with her."

I felt betrayed by the CPS person I had spoken to over the phone; her advice to call the police put me back into my mom's hands.

I think about moms who have their children taken away for leaving them in a car for a few minutes or for letting them wander outside unattended. How was my mom able to get the courts, the law, on her side over and over again?

I thought, *how far would I have to let this go?* Maybe if I had a broken arm instead of enduring abandonment and mental abuse, they would have had enough evidence. Maybe I should have let her beat me with my lamp so I could show them what she was capable of. I could tell them, "This is what I look like on the inside too."

For the second time in my life, I was forced to go with my mom after she'd come back after abandoning me; this time I was scared for different reasons. I was scared because I knew her not from a picture, but for who she really was.

I willed myself to remain calm as I got into the car. My mom chain-smoked as we drove around for hours. It was as if she had picked me up from a study group and we were catching up on the day. Except she said things like, "Why did you abandon me?" and

"You can't possibly believe those people love you" and "What if I drove the car into a tree?"

Eventually, she pulled into the parking lot of a hospital. I felt a glimmer of hope that she was going to check herself back in. Inside we sat down and waited, and after some time her name was called. I picked up a magazine and thumbed through, not seeing the pictures or the articles, but the motion of turning pages anchored me to the moment.

My mom walked out with a doctor and he asked me, "Do you know why you are here?"
I blinked at the vague question and watched my mom as I gave the most generic answer I could muster. "Um, I was staying with my friend and my mom came to pick me up. I don't think she is feeling well so we came here."

My mom let out a hard, short laugh. "She's lying. My daughter is mentally unstable and needs to be checked into the psych ward immediately!" Her voice was shrill, and she waved her hands around for emphasis.

Everyone in the waiting room turned to look at us. I calmly told the doctor, "I'm fine but my mom just got out of a mental institution because she had a breakdown. I thought we were coming in for her." I tried to sound as sane as possible and hoped he believed me because telling someone you aren't crazy usually makes you sound crazy.

He nodded and pulled my mom to the side. "Your daughter seems fine, but I think you should stay for further examination."

As this was happening, a woman came over and slipped a fortune-cookie sized note into my hand. I stuffed it into my pocket as my mom turned away from the doctor; her eyes unfocused. She grabbed my arm and pulled me toward the exit. Nobody tried to stop us, even as I looked back pleadingly.

Later I read that note. The woman had written, *I will pray for you.*

My mom drove around a bit longer, finally pulling into a shopping center to use a payphone. She shuffled through coins in her console and it seemed like she would never find a quarter.

I fought the urge to escape as I watched her dial but didn't move a muscle. I was worried she was calling my sister and if I left, she'd be stuck in that passenger seat instead. My mom got back into the car and we sat as she lit cigarette after cigarette. I watched the butts smolder in the overflowing ashtray.

I stared out the window as people strode by, chatting and laughing, shopping bags hanging from their arms. I thought about fogging up the window and writing HELP ME.

Finally, through the haze of smoke that filled the car I saw two familiar faces. At first, I thought I'd imagined them but still threw open the car door as they walked in my direction. My stepdad's parents had come to take me home with them. My mom had ripped me from a safe space, tried to commit me, and was now leaving me with the parents of the man who had left me to fend for myself.

I was lucky, though, because they were kind and I knew I would be safe with them. But the situation felt deranged; I felt drained. I would end up staying with them for a few weeks, missing school, until my friend's parents somehow worked out an agreement with my mom. She would allow them to become my *in loco parentis*.

My mom knew she couldn't take care of me, but she still needed to control my fate. She wouldn't allow me to leave her unless she granted the permission. Even though CPS did nothing to help me, there was now a record of her being in the institution, of me having called CPS.

Fresh from building her own case against the university (and losing), she could see how events might turn against her. By giving the other family permission to keep me, she wasn't losing me. She was still in control.

34

I entered my junior year of high school in this new home, relieved to be out of a volatile space. I stepped into a family that I had only dreamed of being a part of. Loving parents, a warm home, dinner as a family, and church on Sundays. I felt detached from my other life and I felt safe.

I was making space to be the person I had always wanted to be and to live the life I dreamed of. I didn't talk much about why I moved out of my home. Our friends just accepted it and the other kids at school didn't really ask. It was just like we were embarking on the longest sleepover ever. This was fun! I didn't want anyone to feel sorry for me. I didn't want to be a *Debbie Downer*. So, I tried to only let myself *really* cry when I was alone. But if I needed comfort- a hug or a long conversation was always ready for me.

I signed up for cross country in the fall and track in the winter. I always loved running and was over the fear of shattering my left heel bone. Being part of a team taught me about relationships and sportsmanship. I was part of a group and we rooted for each other's success, but also worked autonomously toward our own goals. I made friends outside my group of friends and felt happy as my world continued to expand.

My *new* family was Catholic, and I, too, had been raised as such for a period of time. In the chaos of my life, I didn't know if or when I had been baptized, and in the moment, it felt very important that I do so. I wanted to fully integrate with my *new* family plus many of our friends were Catholic too. I was also feeling lost and looked toward God for answers. I found peace in the experience. My best friend (really like my sister now) became my "sponsor" and we would go to class every Tuesday where I studied up on the religion and prepared for my confirmation and baptism. I even got to pick my confirmation name. I chose Mary.

I continued to excel in school, tripling up on GT and AP math and science classes, alongside AP English. I was popular *and* nerdy. I was dating hot guys. I seemed to have the whole package.

We were still teenagers though and we would go to parties. It was exciting and fun to sip the warm beers the older kids would bring. Sometimes a bottle of liquor would surface, and we smoked cigarettes. There was a place we called McTacoHut because it encompassed the three fast food joints. If there was nothing to do or if a party broke up, people would gather there to grab 99-cent burritos or French fries. We would sit in the parking lot and chat for hours. We didn't have pagers or cell phones yet. This is how we found each other.

A friend had a van and one day we all piled in and headed to a Dave Matthews concert. It was the first concert we had gone to by ourselves and we were excited. We stocked up on cheap beer and wine. We grossly underestimated how bad traffic would be getting there versus our need to pee. We laughed and threw bagels at each other as we took turns peeing in an empty fast food cup. When we finally reached the concert, we found more friends, kids from a year and two above us. One of the older girls could see how drunk we were, and she taught us how to make ourselves throw up. Throw up so you can have more fun!

I did try to find my dad but all I remembered was my grandma Emma's address in Ohio and his name. That address was burned in my memory. We didn't have email or Internet yet, so I wrote letters. I didn't hear back, and I wasn't sure that I ever would.

During the summer of 1997, I secured a job as a hostess at the newly opened Silver Diner. My *new* parents were generously paying for stuff that I needed and treated me as their own daughter, but I wanted to be as little of a burden as possible. I had always been at least a little financially independent with my babysitting and had the need to earn my own money. I worked at the diner through my senior year and after graduation, climbing my way up from hostess to soda jerk to expo to server. I met people from all ages and backgrounds. It opened my eyes to a broader world around me.

When my mom and stepdad's divorce was finalized (again) toward the end of the year, I was given his 1988 Toyota Celica as part of the agreement. It had been a far sexier sports car in its heyday, but I was thrilled! It was the first time I felt like I had something that was really mine. My friends had their cars for a year.

Once, we got in trouble for smoking cigarettes and we had both of our car keys taken away. It was the only time I stepped out of line and I panicked at the gravity of emotion that swept over me. I couldn't handle the normal consequences a teenager should experience. I felt ashamed of my actions, afraid they would want me to move out, and desperate to hold onto the one thing that could help me physically escape should my mom come back for me.

35

It came time to apply for colleges and I got into a few. I was so excited to start this new journey of my life and really make something of myself. I lettered in academia and had received an Army ROTC scholarship to help pay for university.

A classmate and I had both applied for the scholarship, putting hours into our applications and essays. My friend's dad had taken us for our physical exams all the way out in Maryland. I wanted to serve my country *and* get a quality education. This was everything I had worked so hard for.

I got the scholarship. But my dreams were quickly shot down, one by one. I realized that the Army ROTC scholarship would only partially cover my tuition, so I would have to apply for financial aid. To do that, I needed my parents' information and I only had my mom at the time. Also, I wouldn't turn eighteen until after the college school year started. I had started on the early side when I was in kindergarten, which left me always a few months behind my peers.

My mom refused to fill out the paperwork. I begged and pleaded for weeks. I complimented her and screamed at her and cried in front of her. She refused. It was the most dangerous and harmful move she had ever made on me. It nearly broke me.

I started doing research to see if I could take out my own loans, but I was only seventeen. And even if I was eighteen, there were restrictions around student loans and bank loans for large sums of money.

So, despite having been accepted into several schools and working so hard to get the Army ROTC scholarship, I had to accept the fact that I must take a different path. I had a few friends who were going to stay in the area to work, go to community college, and get an apartment. So that became my plan as well. I could get a year under my belt, save some money, and then qualify for some type of loans once I turned eighteen.

I geared up to take finals in a few weeks, telling myself, *you can do this.*

36

It was the month of my senior finals. I was seventeen. I was a virgin. I was raped.

To this day, I can't listen to Dave Matthews without remembering that night. Also, there is a cologne that the guy wore that I can identify from a mile away.

I was dating a guy that I met at the Silver Diner. I had made a group of friends. We all went to different schools and had fun party hopping, meeting new people, and exploring a world outside of our own high schools.

The month leading up to my assault, I was still feeling optimistic about life despite the crippling blow that I would have to defer university attendance. I had money in my pocket, a car, and was always up for an adventure with friends. It was the best of times.

I was dating a nice guy and I liked hanging out with him. But then we became physical and he wanted sex and I didn't. One night we were at a party. It was early and we snuck away to make out. He started to poke and prod and when I stopped him, things went downhill. He wanted sex, and again I didn't feel ready. We broke things off on the spot and went to go find our friends and enjoy the rest of the party.

About a week later, his handsome prep school friend started talking to me. It began innocently, with a cigarette on the deck. He sympathized with what a jerk my ex had been. He grabbed a few beers and said, "Let's go somewhere else".

He took me to a clearing, where he played Dave Matthews "Crash" and we danced in the moonlight. It felt gentle and romantic. I was wearing my favorite silver anklet that night and it got lost somewhere in that field.

We went back to our friend's house, and by then everyone had left or was cozying up somewhere. I was not sure where my friends were. Having not driven there, it looked like I would have to crash for the night. We sat on the couch and then he kissed me. He got on top of me.

I was wearing a skirt, and he started fingering me as we kissed. I was tipsy and this suddenly seemed to be going too fast. I started to wiggle in order to get away from him and then he moved with lightning speed.

Both of his hands were suddenly pinning my arms down and I felt something pressing and hard inside of me. When I looked into his eyes and said "No," he flipped me on my stomach, pulled my underwear all the way down, and tried to anally penetrate me.

I cried out in pain and he said, "See, it's better the other way. Just relax." Then he thrust into me, pressing my face into the cushion. He insisted that I should be appreciative that he was penetrating me the *normal* way. I was *told* that this felt good.

When my muffled screams for him to stop threatened to alert others, he got up in disgust and said, "You don't know what you're missing." He threw a blanket over me and left.

I remained on my stomach in the dark, my underwear around my ankles. It took me awhile before I managed to pull them back up. I barely slept. He paged me the next day and when I called him back, he sounded sweet, as if I meant something special to him. For a long time, that's how I tried to shape the narrative. He was a wealthy,

Catholic boy from a good family. He couldn't have *really* raped me, right?

For months afterward, we continued to hang out. I told myself that I was his girlfriend and went running to him anytime he asked. But he treated me horribly, and I was starting to self-medicate with alcohol and drugs. One night, I broke down and confessed the assault to a friend.

I finally told Prep School Guy that I knew he raped me and that he was using me. I told him that I never wanted to see him again. Then the stalking began, which went on for over a year. He would come to my work or find out where I was. He got off on the power of seeing me completely fall apart at the sight of him. My fear turned to anger, and I told *everybody* what really happened. Alarmingly, the guys nodded. They knew he liked to take advantage of intoxicated girls.

Years later, he apologized to me at a bar. I watched him approach me, my heart racing as he asked if he could talk to me. I listened to him speak and felt validated to hear him admit that he had raped me.

Recently, I looked him up on Facebook and he is married with kids. I still have trouble with people touching me.

37

I was emotionally, mentally, and now physically bruised. I was entering the real world, not even yet a legal adult. I couldn't lean on those who did try to love me because I didn't trust that anymore. I even pulled away from my friend's parents who had taken me in. Understandably they couldn't help me with college, and I felt like a failure and an embarrassment- even though it wasn't my fault.

I was about to turn eighteen, working three jobs, and going to school full time at the community college. I was smart, pretty, and completely damaged. I had everything and nothing going for me. I showed one personality in public, but underneath the surface I lurked in my shadow.

One day I came across the only sentimental thing my mom had ever given me. It was a silver charm bracelet with a Saint Christopher Medal, the patron saint of travelers. Her mom had given it to her and at some point, she passed it down to me.

While journaling one night, I felt like I needed to do something that would mean something, that might make her feel the seriousness of my pain. I took the only thing she had ever given me and put it into a plastic bag. I didn't include a note but figured she would know what is was, and who it was from.

A raging storm had crept in and I could barely see through the wipers as I headed to my mom's house. I could see and feel the lightning and thunder. It pulsated through my veins. When I pulled up to her house, I rolled down the window and threw the bag at her door, any clanking noise of metal hitting the sidewalk inaudible against the thunder.

On my eighteenth birthday, everyone was away at college, except for those of us who stayed behind. Another friend's parents had me over for dinner and cake that week to celebrate. I had a quick call with my sister and all I could feel was the falseness of the promises I made to her before. Turning eighteen was not enough fuel to fight a custody battle against my mom. I had been naive to think I could save her.

To pass the day (and numb this pain), I decided to get my tongue pierced. I thought this act of rebellion could be shocking and life changing. I remember feeling so on edge. *What was this life? Where was I going? What is there to experience?* I dialed up on AOL, found a tattoo and piercing parlor, and printed out directions.

I felt fearless, sitting in the chair as the piercer clamped my tongue. I watched her, cross-eyed, as she slid the rod through my tongue and then screwed on the peridot (my birthstone) encrusted ball on top. Surprisingly, this did not hurt at all. It would be painful for days after that, the swelling slurring my words as I waited tables, my customers wondering if I was drunk or had some type of affliction.

I enjoyed the pain though. I liked feeling something, that I was forced to feel that something. I couldn't hide this physical pain like I could emotional pain. I had to experience it, deal with it, acknowledge it. It somehow made me feel alive and present, not numb and fading into the darkness. Piercings and tattoos would become part of my survival toolkit. If something bad happened and I felt myself fading, I would get one to spark me back to life. I looked at the tools laid out on the side table and would feel a rush of relief. They were like defibrillators, bringing me back to life.

There was a 24-hour diner down the street from where I worked. We would go after our shift, always sitting in the same section with the same waitress who never remembered us. We called her *fish lady* because fish lose their memories every twenty-four hours. Just once I wished she returned a smile or had a flash of recognition.

It made me sad because it felt like life was so heavy for her that she couldn't bring herself to engage, even when someone was smiling wide for her. Or maybe she just thought we were jerk kids, smoking and drinking coffee during all hours of the night. Maybe she hated cigarettes and resented having to dump our ashtray every twenty minutes because *two butts, too much* and it seemed like we were double fisting, in a smoking contest, just to fill that ashtray up for her to dump.

The times I was hungry, I would order steak and eggs and slather my food with A1 sauce. I felt grown up to have my own money. It felt powerful, even though the steak was stringy and tough and the eggs just a simple scramble. It was a special treat I provided for myself.

38

I smoked cigarettes and drank my mom's cheap liquor when I was thirteen years old, when we lived in Mobile, but I didn't carry those habits with me to Virginia. I remember smoking a few cigarettes and splitting a beer occasionally freshman and sophomore year. Junior and senior year, we had weekend parties, but the partying was minimal. It was normal, social use and I never felt like I *needed* anything. We were all athletes and in AP/GT classes and cared about our bodies and our futures.

It's easy to say that kids experimenting with drinking and smoking weed is the gateway to trying harder drugs. There is a case for that. I probably wouldn't have tried ecstasy if I had never smoked weed. I would have never tried weed if I hadn't drank. I wouldn't have smoked cigarettes if I didn't drink, and maybe I wouldn't have done any of those things if my mom didn't have them easily accessible around the house. I wouldn't have touched those things if *she* had actually been in the house. Maybe she would have been home more if she was mentally and emotionally healthy, if she really loved and cared about our well-being.

The *what if* game.

Within a couple of short months, I lost the two things that I thought I had control over, that I had fought for, that I loved and cherished—my future and my body.

I experienced these things and thought this was what life really was like. There will be no fairy tale ending to my story. There will always be someone there who will take it away, try to destroy me. And I asked myself so many times, *why did they do this?*

I made a new group of friends within the local rave culture, and they lived in a loft apartment in the suburbs of DC. Every Friday, they would convene, leaving day jobs and weekday selves behind. It was exactly what the shadow within me needed.

When I first walked into the apartment, I felt an immediate sense of *hell yeah*. To the left, there was a kitchen and a small dining room space. To the right was a living room with a high ceiling and a fireplace. A loft peeked over the living room and someone waved down to me. Directly ahead was a hallway with a bathroom and a bedroom. I would spend most of my time in the loft and living room. There was a deck, but we chain-smoked freely in the apartment.

The first time I hung out with them, we started the pregame by smoking some weed and cigarettes. Drinking was not a big part of our lives then. I scanned the room and took in the tight T-shirts and baggy pants, the rainbow bracelets, and the binkies hanging from string tied around their necks. I took in the bleached-out hair, lava lamps, the stuffed Teletubbies, and the glow sticks. I took in the hugs and the makeup they put on me, eyeliner matching both the boys and girls. I took in meeting these people who were so different from the people I had always known. I felt connected even though I was not sure what I was connecting to yet.

We made our way to a rave in the city. In the car, my new friends described ecstasy to me. They told me how to take it, to drink plenty of water, and advice on how to act normal in front of security. They said the best part is, you get to dance the night away.

When we pulled up, the neighborhood was a bit rough, but we did not care. We walked with ease and excitement. It was my first time going to a club, having recently turned eighteen. The warehouse was dimly lit, as if every corner we passed was filled with secrets. Deep, booming vibrations pumped from the speakers and seemed to seep into the floors and walls. I could feel the music wrap itself around me, with every heartbeat pulsing wildly to the beat. I was now a part of this living, breathing experience. My new friend dropped a pill into my hand and told me that this batch was called "tweety bird." I swallowed and waited.

When it kicked in, I looked up at him with wide, dilated eyes and he smiled down at me. We danced the night away, and I knew I would do it again. The world felt safe and soft. People were touching me, and I did not recoil. I wanted more hugs, more dancing, and more massages. I thought I would explode with happiness. In that moment, I didn't need to remember that my dreams of university had been shattered, or that my body had been violated. All that mattered in the moment was that I was with these beautiful people.

I stayed over that night, and the next and the next. We never really slept on Friday night; we kept the party going into Saturday. Someone went out and bought a huge bag of chicken nuggets and fries from money we had pooled together, and we ate it all. We nestled into the apartment and wandered happily into Saturday night. These people were amazing. *I* felt amazing.

On Sunday, someone decided we should do acid. I thought, *if they do it, then I will too.*

It was terrifying. I had spent the past two days doing ecstasy for the first time and loving it. But my body was tired and hungry and dehydrated. I should have gone home but I put the paper strip on my tongue and proceeded to have the worst experience of my life.

I stared at the lava lamp. I watched a guy run around saying he was a Tyrannosaurus rex, making his arms small and his stride wide. I went into the loft bathroom and took a shower. I watched my skin melt off my body and I stared deep into the mirror, into the eyes of the shadow that lurked beneath the surface.

Someone gave me a rainbow-colored stuffed caterpillar. I rubbed the caterpillar's nose on my own and it helped center me.

I finally decided it was enough and that I would die if I did not leave. I called a friend and he immediately came to meet me. I was not quite sober at this point but in my panic the only solution was for me to follow him in my car back to his mom's house. We made it safely and it was late, but his mom was up. He told her that I had gone through a bad breakup and needed a friend and a place to stay. She made me food, which I surprisingly devoured. She made me a bed on the couch and tucked me in and hugged me goodnight.

I was hooked and would start going out with the ravers every weekend (I would never touch acid again though). Something exciting happened one weekend- my first girl kiss. She wasn't one of my straight girlfriends who would drunkenly kiss me in the years to come. She was a stranger that I met at a lesbian bar in the city. We had taken a detour from our normal rave parties. In this life, of raves and PLUR, groups of people intersected and doors to new worlds were opening faster than I could enter, stay, or settle into the space. I stood in the foyer and craned my neck to see down the hallway but usually didn't get much further than that. This night, I would get further than that.

The bar was dark and sticky, and smelled of freshly popped popcorn. The hot steam breathed from the machines, creating a dreamy effect. The women pressed against each other, some dancing and some making out. I wondered if any of them had boyfriends waiting at home. Would they say that they had been at the movies? Next to cocktail napkins, there were pencils and small blank business cards so women could exchange numbers, find each other outside these secret walls.

Before I knew it, I was swaying back and forth with a girl who looked at me with wide, wanting eyes. Then we were kissing, and she was kissing me like she wanted to be a part of me, not like she was painting herself on my lips for the boys to see. It was exciting and I felt a flash of desire burn hot across my body as I pulled her by the waist, closer to me. But then again, everything felt good to the touch. Ecstasy had a way of doing that to a person.

We had to go, and she grabbed a pencil. She slipped her number to me and I carefully took it like it was a receipt, proof that night had happened and in case I needed to return it later. It was a bold suggestion that there was a gay life outside of these club walls and that we might want to see each other. I tucked the tiny card into my purse, into a pocket where the memory of that night would slumber for years. Conjuring the smell of popcorn when I pressed it to my lips.

Another night, I sat cross-legged in front of a mirror we had taken off the living room wall. My friend winked at me as he finished tapping a credit card against the mirror where thick powdery lines spelled my initials: MM. I took a deep breath, made sure the bill was tightly rolled, and leaned down.

I inhaled the lines the same way one blows out all their birthday candles in one breath. *My wish* was to escape the part of me that felt, thought, and had to responsibly interact with the outside world. I felt my brain awaken the *better* part of me. Anxiety melted away. I had stories to tell, people to meet, and songs to dance to. I was ready for an adventure and life felt full of promise as we headed into the night.

A friend's brother was asleep on the couch. I was in the loft and thought I smelled something a bit strange. I looked down and saw the couch on fire—someone must have dropped their cigarette between the cushions. I saw the small flames flicker by his feet as he slept. I yelled down to those in the living room, pulling them out of their deep moments. There was a little panic and laughter as they woke him up, put the fire out, and turned the cushion over. Then everyone went back to what they were doing.

The guy that I ended up dating had claimed the loft for his bedroom. There was a connecting bathroom and a guitar case full of drugs. We had everything we needed in that room.

As the daylight would creep up on us, we resisted and covered the large windows with thick blankets and huddled together in the loft. We would pop more pills, do more lines, smoke more weed. We had a large bottle of cheap liquor to take off the edge if we ran out of our drug supply, but that rarely happened. Some nights, it would just be him and I hooking up as we rode the roller coaster of our roll. Sometimes, people were spread across the floor giving massages and rubbing Vicks Vapor Rub on each other.

I've only been pulled over twice in my life and they were both during this time, of me racing to drive to the apartment where my friends were waiting for me. I raced from hours of classes, work, and homework to go to the place where I could melt into the couch and relax. One time, I couldn't talk myself out of the ticket for popping a U-turn but the other, and worse, infraction I lucked out. I had been going about twenty miles over the speed limit at midnight, my

Toyota Celica looking slick and sporty, the pale pink masked in the darkness.

I conjured up tears and by the end of our conversation, the cop had a sympathetic look in his eyes as he told me that *breakups are tough, remember to buckle up,* and *to drive home safely.* The next day, I cleaned my ashtray of the roaches and made sure every baggie and loose pill was gone. I had entered the stage of knowing that I was playing with my future and was starting to question if I should continue.

A couple of months later, I walked into a drug raid at the apartment and the decision was made for me. We were handcuffed and told to sit on the couch. They tore up the apartment around us as we sat still and quiet, the eye of the hurricane. We were questioned and our cars searched. We were finally let go because they didn't find anything. It was a Tuesday night and we were just there to watch a movie.

I was done with the rave scene. Most of us were and retreated to where we came from. Some of us stayed in touch immediately after and some of us found each other years later social media. Except for one of our friends, who died of a heroin overdose. Our sweet friend, who would wear fairy wings and dance for us during the late hours of the night. It was numbing to hear that news. It felt like I was a different person already, and the old me was receiving and processing, somewhere in the background where I couldn't see her cry.

39

I made a new best friend, Marina. She was a beautiful girl with big eyes and thick curly hair. I would watch her talk, her lips as she licked a blunt closed. Every movement was captivating to me and when she would speak, I felt I would do anything she said.

We smoked a lot of weed. Like a lot. Sometimes we would get ecstasy pills. One night we were chatting, and she asked, "Do you have a vibrating egg?" I had no idea what she was talking about and she told me how good it felt to take a pill and then use that on yourself. She suggested that I go buy one and that we would take pills together, and then use them. I was stunned but tried to act cool. Marina came from a different culture. She told me of stories back home where women would be free with each other behind closed doors, when the men weren't around. She told me about how she lived through war, how she killed poisonous snakes in outhouses with her bare hands. I believed everything she said, so I went and bought this vibrating egg.

We drove out to a remote place, car stocked with water and weed, and two tiny pills pressing against the fabric of my small right jean pocket.

We took the pills, chugged some water, smoked a bit, and then talked about life, love, religion, and everything else. As it started to kick in hard, she looked at me, leaned into her glove compartment and took out her egg. "Did you bring yours?" she asked. I did.

And she was right. It felt incredible.

40

I tried to mend my relationship with my mom. I would pop over for brief visits. I even went to Thanksgiving in 1999. It had even seemed nice.

I found out that my mom got married to a man only a few years older than me. My sister had found out from reading mail that had come in. Mom's last name now reflecting that of the guy she had been dating. Jill had moved back in at some point but tried not to be home. I tried to be there for her as much as I could but was working a few jobs and in school.

I found out that my sister had been sleeping in her car, in the winter. Things had gotten bad at home and she hadn't told anyone, but finally broke down and told me. My mom hadn't raised alarm that she hadn't seen my sister for weeks. I was in a rage and went to the house.

Her new husband was there and as I confronted my mom, he spoke in a condescendingly quiet voice for me to calm down. I told him that he was not part of our family and had no idea what we had been through with her.

She just stood there with no expression on her face. She asked me why I cared so much, I was the one who had abandoned the family. She said this to me often and I tried to ignore her, to not believe her. This time I just saw red though and I believe I would have hit her but somehow, I restrained myself. I had never felt a rage so deep before. My sister was displaced by this man who came into the home from nowhere. She was sleeping in her car in the freezing weather. Did my mom have *any* ability to feel guilt, shame, or worry?

That was the last time I would ever see my mom.

41

My phone rang, and I looked at the caller ID. I wasn't expecting to hear from the private eye after only three days. I was now twenty-one and decided to find my dad. I had randomly selected this detective's name from the Yellow Pages and called to tentatively ask if he could help me. It felt odd, just calling. I felt like I was supposed to have this movie moment where I walked into someone's office, wearing a trench coat and a hat, everything in black and white, as jazz music played in the background.

I would breathlessly say, "I haven't seen my dad in twelve years. Can you help me?" Instead, my private eye simply answered the phone and asked me for information about my dad. I shared the only two things I knew: my dad's name and the address in Ohio.

As I picked up the phone, I wondered, *what if he doesn't want anything to do with me?* and *I hope he is still alive.*

Secondary questions buzzed: *Where has he been? Why did he stop loving us? Is he still a good hugger?*

He *was* still alive, and we started emailing and talking on the phone when we could. He was remarried now, and I got to know her too. I heard stories of my little brother. My dad booked a flight with borrowed airline miles and came to visit me.

When he walked out of the terminal, he looked smaller than I remembered. Time had done its job on him. He had long gray hair and deep lines on his face. I hesitated for a moment. The woman I had become wanted to shrink and turn into a little girl again. I wanted to run toward him without inhibition and to hug him.

My sister and I sat in my living room with him as he told us stories of our childhood, of what his life was now. We listened to his story about how my mom almost had an abortion because my sister was from an affair. How he convinced her not to. We listened as our hearts burst with sadness and confusion. Did our whole family know this? It turns out they did.

My dad tried to talk to me about what happened, about how hard he looked for us. I wanted to believe him, but I knew he had given up quickly. I wanted to forgive him, so I tried to brush past this conversation. I pushed back the anger and sadness that wanted to consume me. I refrained from saying to him, "I found you in three days, living in remote Alaska. How could you not find me?" The ache to have a *normal* parent in my life was so deep that I was willing to look past all of that. As long as he loved me.

I took my dad to Great Falls and we hiked and talked about life. Me smoking Marlboro Lights and him rolling his own cigarettes. He was quite the philosopher; I could talk to him for hours. He talked about his life in Alaska and living off the land, about his new family.

I would meet them in a few years. The whole family would fly out and I would have a BBQ at my best friend's. My stepmom would tell me she was pregnant with her second child and I would tell her that I was gay. I would ask her to tell my dad for me, as those words were still hard for me to say out loud. I had grown close with her- not quite felt like a daughter, but close to it. But not after my confession. As we hugged each other, I didn't realize that I was celebrating but she already constructing an email in her head. An email that she would send to me later, that let me know being gay was wrong.

My dad shared a document with me during this first meeting. I would hold onto it for fifteen years before I read it. At first, I couldn't bear it, then I just forgot I had it. I found the document in my move out west.

It was neatly typed, with an introduction of how his children were ripped away from him, and his attempts to fight the courts to regain custody. There was a timeline of the events from the first ten years of my life and letters from his friends. They spoke highly of my dad and pleaded with the courts to find my sister and I, for the sake of our well-being. It's incredibly detailed. It was the most I had ever learned of my childhood. It was the most I had ever seen someone talk about me, even if it was just faded ink on paper.

42

Right before finding my dad, I had started dating Tristan. We had met years before, when I was eighteen. He worked at a local coffee shop that would become the center of my universe for the next few years, ingesting caffeine and making friends. Our hodge podge group would read, journal, smoke cigarettes, talk about life for hours and hours.

Tristan always had a little crush on me, but I didn't pay much attention to it. He was younger and kind of goofy, a couple years away from growing into the man that I would find attractive and sweet. But we became close friends and saw each other through some fun, crazy times. Saw each other through relationships and eventually saw each other through a lens other than friendship.

I remember the day that I really noticed him, as potential boyfriend material. We were at my friend's pool birthday party. Over the years, he had really been there for me. He cared about me finding my dad, getting an office job, then getting on track for a real career. I felt safe in his arms when he hugged me. Then I realized that I wanted to stay in those arms for longer than a hug. I wanted to feel them flex as he made love to me. I wanted to feel their weight on me after he drifted to sleep, hear his heartbeat slow down after a night of passion.

When we started dating, the world turned upside down. It was hot and heavy; we were *The Couple*. We spent every night together, partying with friends as much as we stayed at home, drinking wine and making dinner from Costco. It felt so grown up, those nights, grocery shopping and cooking together.

We had a strong relationship, but we also fought. There was jealousy and suspicion. We were both too attractive for our own good, too hot headed for our own good. We loved each other too intensely. I picked fights with Tristan because I had something gnawing deep inside of me, something I had no name for yet. It made me feel terrible.

We dated for three years and got to a point where our friends started taking their relationships to the next level, moving in and getting married. I felt the world closing in around me, and I broke up with him and moved to North Carolina. I had no explanation for what I was doing but I felt like it was do or die, and I wasn't ready to die yet.

It was one of the hardest things I have ever done. I loved him; I still have love for him. He is kind, smart, and hilarious. We remain friends and I hope we always will. It took us a few years after the breakup to start speaking again. It must have been hard for him when I came out. It was hard for me to tell him. But we were friends from the beginning and had a loving foundation. He gave me a sense of security that I had not felt from a man before, and I am forever grateful for that.

43

I moved back home after a five-month stint of beach life, and what some might call a mid-twenties crisis. My friend, Morgan, and I had moved to North Carolina, just before our birthdays in August. Now I headed back, in a snowstorm in the middle of December.

North Carolina had been good for me. I had figured out more about my life in those short months than I had in years. I needed that time away to allow me to break up with my long-time boyfriend, step away from the party scene, and the long hours at the office. I had been burning the candle at both ends.

As I packed, something interesting happened. Morgan sat by my side and noted that it was time for me to declutter. She made me throw out my old cassette tapes, boxes of junk, and old furniture. As I was going through one of the boxes, I came across a card with a girl's name scribbled above a phone number. I suddenly remembered the first girl I had kissed six years earlier in the lesbian club, the smell of popcorn surrounding us. That recollection awakened something in me. I had kissed girls since then, but *that* memory made me feel something, like I had the answer to everything on the tip of my tongue.

Shortly after I moved back, I found myself at my friend Violet's place. We drank wine like we always did but this night was different. My skin prickled as she brushed past me, her eyebrows raised when I shared my thoughts of women with her. She looked beautiful as she talked about the one time, *she* had dated a girl.

I encouraged her to describe her experience and soon we found ourselves aroused. We kissed, clothes falling off our bodies, and I didn't hesitate once as we went all the way. It was like the thunder that followed lightning, the storm that I had been waiting for. I had been counting, one Mississippi, two Mississippi, three Mississippi for an eternity and now my body crackled with sensation. I was electrified.

I found myself on MySpace staring at the "sexual orientation" box. I chewed on my lip as I dropped down the list selection to "lesbian." I took a deep breath and picked up my phone. I had a lot of phone calls to make and people to see. *This* was happening.

People's reactions to me coming out:

Friends: Duh.

Sister: Cool.

Grandma Grace: You no gay, you Catholic! I love you.

Mom: That's great. Do you have a girlfriend?

Cousin: Me too.

Other family: We love you.

My stepmom: I don't judge, Jesus judges.

Dad: How's the weather there?

The next few years, I did try to have a relationship with my parents. I wanted them to apologize for my tumultuous childhood and to accept me for who I was. But I couldn't get that from either of them, and I was exhausted from trying. My sister also pulled away from me for reasons of her own. I am not sure if she ever recovered from the news my dad had told us about her birth. I can speculate that she resented me, that a depression took her over, that she felt left out of this new life I had built. But they are her reasons, and I've lived a decade with no answers.

I have many emails, going back and forth with my parents over the years and it's the same conversation repeatedly. They both seem open and ready to build a relationship, then in the next round of emails we escalate to the same issues. They seem to have different recollections of what transpired, and I have found myself in a loop. I feel like I will always be a child asking, *why didn't you love me?* I try to say, *I forgive you, why can't you love me now?*

It had taken me too long to come out. I can say it's because I didn't have access to gay role models or communities. That I was so busy trying to be a perfect image of what I thought others wanted that I completely and wholly ignored this part of me. That I didn't grow up in an emotionally safe space where I could even explore the feelings that had always been there.

The hardest thing about my dad is that I was supposed to take so many things on good faith and forgive and accept what happened to me and his failings. I succeeded and thrived in life despite everything, because I had turned out to be not only a decent human, but really caring and kind.

But he couldn't accept me being gay. He talked about loving me no matter what, but the judgment was there.

My mom's responses always follow the same format. *Sorry I haven't reached out, but I have been sick.* Once she apologized for never holding me or making eye contact with me as a baby. That her Asperger's prevented her from bonding with me. *I love you*; she wrote once. It was the only time she ever shared those three words with me. But as soon as she seems ready to open and I feel a glimmer of hope, she will say something cruel. I feel like an abandoned, scared child again.

In order to find some type of happiness, I knew that I needed to break the cycle of trying to reconcile with them. If I was being honest with myself, I was fatigued from acting as a parent or a forgiving child. I wanted to explore my new life, free of burden and judgment from my family. The next few years, I gained a new family to replace then one I had lost.

I saw a therapist, a psychologist, for quite some time. I said out loud the events of my life and he bore witness to what I experienced, and for the first time I felt seen. I began to see parts of myself for the first time and at times I cry, because what I see is beautiful and it hurts me. It's hard to understand that I have been so cruel and unforgiving to myself for something other people did to me.

I read books, I write, and I heal. I feel like I have a fighting chance, but first I needed to acknowledge what I experienced growing up, to grieve my losses, and to let my parents both go.

To them I say, *I love you, and goodbye.*

About the Author

Persephone Grey is a poet, writer, and author of the new memoir *The Girl Who Wasn't me*. Her coming-of-age memoir follows the journey of her parents' erratic lifestyles, what it was like to have a mom with undiagnosed autistic spectrum disorder, and the struggle to understand her sexuality. Persephone has been a lifelong writer, as journaling was her anchor amongst the chaos. She currently lives in San Francisco with her dog, Chuck, a Shiba-Inu/ Chihuahua mix who looks like a small fox.

Made in the USA
Middletown, DE
21 July 2019